Aviation Elite Units

No 617
'Dambusters' Sqn

No 617 'Dambusters' Sqn

Alex Bateman
Series editor Tony Holmes

Front Cover

As the main wave of No 617 Sqn aircraft headed towards the Möhne Dam during the final hours of 16 May 1943, several came under fire along the way, including Flt Lt John Hopgood's ED925/AJ-M, which was raked by flak along its length. The ground fire left the Lancaster's port outer engine ablaze and injured several of the crew, including Hopgood himself, who sustained a head wound. Flight engineer Flt Sgt Charles Brennan tended to his skipper, exclaiming 'Christ, look at the blood'. Having been patched up, Hopgood feathered the now useless port outer engine, dousing the flames.

Arriving at the Möhne, Wg Cdr Guy Gibson, squadron commander and pilot of ED932/AJ-G, turned in to make his attack. Having dropped his mine short of the target, he passed over the dam and climbed away. Hopgood was called in next, and at 0032 hrs he too turned to make his attacking run.

As the damaged Lancaster headed towards the target, the flak gunners on the dam found their range and their shells struck home, setting both port engines and the wing fuel tanks alight. This in turn caused the bomb aimer, Plt Off John Fraser, to drop the mine slightly late. As the crippled aircraft continued on over the dam, Hopgood realised that his situation was hopeless. He struggled to maintain sufficient height to enable some of the crew to try and escape, rear gunner Plt Off Tony Burcher recalling the desperate shout from his wounded pilot;

'Get out you damn fool. If only I could get another 300 ft. I can't get any more height.'

As Fraser bailed out, Burcher helped the severely injured wireless operator Flt Sgt John Minchin to escape before the Lancaster began to disintegrate. Burcher was thrown clear as the bomber finally broke up and crashed several miles from the dam, with four of the crew still aboard (*Cover artwork by Mark Postlethwaite*)

First published in Great Britain in 2009 by Osprey Publishing, Midland House, West Way, Botley, Oxford OX2 0PH, UK
443 Park Avenue South, New York, NY 10016, USA
E-mail; info@ospreypublishing.com

A CIP catalogue record for this book is available from the British Library

ISBN 13: 978 1 84603 429 9
E-book ISBN: 978 1 84908 105 4

Edited by Tony Holmes
Page design by Mark Holt
Cover artwork by Mark Postlethwaite
Aircraft profiles by Chris Davey
Index by Alan Thatcher

Printed and bound in China through Bookbuilders

FOR A CATALOGUE OF ALL BOOKS PUBLISHED BY OSPREY MILITARY AND AVIATION PLEASE CONTACT:

Osprey Direct, c/o Random House Distribution Center, 400 Hahn Road, Westminster, MD 21157
Email: uscustomerservice@ospreypublishing.com

Osprey Direct, The Book Service Ltd, Distribution Centre, Colchester Road, Frating Green, Colchester, Essex, CO7 7DW
Email: customerservice@ospreypublishing.com

www.ospreypublishing.com

09 10 11 12   10 9 8 7 6 5 4 3 2 1

Imperial War Museum Collections
Many of the photos in this book come from the Imperial War Museum's huge collections which cover all aspects of conflict involving Britain and the Commonwealth since the start of the twentieth century. These rich resources are available online to search, browse and buy at www.iwmcollections.org.uk. In addition to Collections Online, you can visit the Visitor Rooms where you can explore over eight million photographs, thousands of hours of moving images, the largest sound archive of its kind in the world, thousands of diaries and letters written by people in wartime, and a huge reference library. To make an appointment, call (020) 7416 5320, or e-mail mail@iwm.org.uk.

Imperial War Museum www.iwm.org.uk

CONTENTS

INTRODUCTION

Prior to the commencement of World War 2, the British Air Staff had drawn up plans for a strategic bombing campaign that was to be implemented in the event of conflict in Europe. One of the key targets identified for the Royal Air Force (RAF) was the German war industry. The plans highlighted powerplants and factories located in the Ruhr area that were considered to be vital to the production of arms and munitions. If these were disabled Germany's ability to produce such items could be brought to a near standstill.

In July 1938 the specific problem of attacking dams was discussed, as they provided the source of hydroelectric power for the Ruhr factories. Four dams in particular were noted as being of great importance – the Möhne, Eder, Sorpe and Enneppe, with the first two alone holding some 336,000,000 tons of water when their respective reservoirs were full. The problem facing the Air Staff was exactly how to attack them.

To begin with, the aircraft, bombs and bombsights then in use by the RAF were inadequate for pinpoint operations. Dams provided a very small target from above, while attacking them from over the water at low-level was fraught with danger. Floats stretched across the reservoirs prevented any attempt by a surface weapon, while huge steel nets suspended beneath them denied any attack by torpedo or mini submarine. They seemed almost impregnable.

At the same time as the Air Staff was discussing methods of attack, the problem was being investigated by Dr Barnes Wallis, the Assistant Chief Designer at Vickers-Armstrong Aviation. He was already well known in aviation circles, having designed the famous R 100 airship in the late 1920s. Wallis was also famous for developing the French geodetic framework, which he used in the construction of the Wellington and Wellesley bombers. He reasoned that by destroying the dams, and in turn the power source for the Ruhr, the thousands of tons of bombs that were being dropped on German factories in this region could be saved. Wallis initially had an idea for a ten-tonne 'earthquake' bomb, which, after being dropped, would reach supersonic speeds before burying itself in the earth and exploding. The resulting shockwave would literally shake down the target. However, the development of this weapon was hampered by the fact that no aircraft was then available to carry it. Undeterred, Wallis simply designed one!

Although seeing some merit in the idea of an 'earthquake bomb' when it was presented to them, the Air Staff never fully backed the project, arguing that putting so much effort into the construction of an aircraft that could carry only a single weapon, at the expense of other projects, was not practical. Wallis abandoned the idea a short while later.

However, although naturally disappointed, he still believed that destroying the source of energy so vital to war production was worth pursuing, and throughout 1940 and into 1941 he conducted tests on model dams. These proved that if a bomb was dropped in the water some distance from the dam wall, the force of the explosion would be dissipated by the water in between. However, if a bomb could be laid right against the wall, the water would instead work in its favour and concentrate the force of the blast through it. This also meant that a far smaller charge would be needed to cause a breach, and in turn a smaller bomb – one that could possibly be carried by an aircraft such as the Avro Lancaster, which had recently entered RAF service. Convinced an explosion in contact with the dam wall was the answer, Wallis set about trying to find a method of delivery.

Aware of the various defensive measures employed by the Germans to protect their dams, Wallis looked into the possibility of using ricochet as a method of delivery. To achieve this, a weapon would have to be dropped at such a height that instead of sinking when it hit the water it would skip across the surface towards the target. After hitting the dam, the bomb would sink, before exploding at a predetermined depth.

In April 1942 Wallis began to test this theory, initially in his back garden using his daughter's marbles, and later at the National Physical Laboratory at Teddington, west of London, where he spent the next three months firing machined spheres up and down the huge ship testing tanks. In late 1942 Wallis gained permission to convert Wellington III BJ895 so that it could carry two inert spherical mines, which it duly dropped at Chesil Beach, off the south coast, in a series of trials that commenced in December 1942 and continued into January 1943.

Wallis envisaged two versions of the weapon. The first, codenamed *Upkeep*, could be used against dams, canals and other static targets, and a smaller version, named *Highball*, could be deployed against shipping.

It is interesting to note that unknown to Wallis, the RAF had already conducted near identical tests with fully armed weapons before he began his own. The Coastal Command Development Unit (CCDU) had wanted to explore different methods of attacking submarines and shipping, and it too looked into the ricochet technique. On 23 August 1942, a CCDU Sunderland dropped six Mk VII depth charges off Troon, on the west coast of Scotland. The tests were moderately successful, although it was concluded that a faired version of the weapon would probably have better range and be more effective. Such drops were never officially used in action, and the tests remained unknown to Wallis.

After the success of his trials, support for Wallis' idea gained momentum. On 26 February 1943, during a meeting at the Ministry of Aircraft Production, the Chairman, Air Marshal Frederick Linnell, announced that the Chief of the Air Staff, Lord Portal had requested that every endeavour be made to produce both the aircraft and weapons for use by the spring of that year. It was to take priority over all other Vickers projects, and Avro would convert three Lancaster B Is as soon as possible for trials with the full-sized bomb.

The final design for *Upkeep* was cylindrical, with four fuses (three hydrostatic, which worked by water pressure, and a self-destruct fuse which, when armed, would detonate 60 seconds after release) fitted in one end. Weighing 9250 lbs, the bomb was almost 60 inches wide and 50 inches in diameter.

With Wallis now committed to developing the weapon, attention turned to the RAF, and the squadron and crews who would be tasked with employing it in combat.

FORMATION AND TRAINING

The Commander in Chief (C-in-C) Bomber Command, Air Chief Marshal (ACM) Arthur Harris, was reluctant to take a complete squadron from frontline service to carry out the Dams raid, so instead it was decided to form a new one using experienced crews. On 17 March 1943, he wrote to Air Vice Marshal (AVM) the Hon Ralph Cochrane, Commander of No 5 Group, explaining that a weapon had been designed for use against dams, and that a new squadron was to be formed within his group to train with the weapon and then employ it. Five principles were laid down when selecting personnel and equipment, which were as follows;

1. The majority of aircrew were to have completed one or two operational tours and the remainder to be specially selected.
2. Special attention was to be paid to the efficiency of ground officers and in particular the Armament Officer.
3. The groundcrews were to be provided, as far as possible, from group resources, and all were to have experience on Lancaster aircraft.
4. Aircraft were to be provided from existing squadrons, but would later be replaced by specially modified versions of the Lancaster.
5. The squadron was to be given priority over everything else, and all endeavours were to be made to form it into an efficient unit by the earliest possible date.

ACM Arthur 'Bomber' Harris, Commander-in-Chief Bomber Command, in his office at the High Wycombe Headquarters in June 1942. Initially sceptical of Barnes Wallis' 'bouncing bomb', he refused to release a complete squadron for the Dams raid, instead authorising the formation of a new one made up of experienced crews (*IWM Neg No CH5491*)

The commander of No 5 Group, AVM the Hon Ralph Cochrane, seen in January 1944. Cochrane had assumed command of the group in February 1942, and was a close friend and ally of Harris, who himself had commanded No 5 Group for the first 14 months of the war. It was no surprise that when No 617 Sqn was formed in March 1943, it was within No 5 Group. The unit remained here for the rest of the war (*IWM Neg No CH11946*)

The man chosen to form and command 'Squadron X' was 24-year-old Wg Cdr Guy Gibson, a highly experienced pilot who had completed almost 170 operations on both bombers and nightfighters from the first day of the war. Grounded after the Dams raid, he constantly requested a return to operations, until his wish was granted. Gibson was subsequently killed in action during an operation to Rheydt, in Germany, on 19 September 1944 (*Canadian Forces Photograph*)

Wg Cdr Guy Gibson was selected to command the new unit. A very experienced 24-year-old pre-war officer, his first operation had been with Hampden I-equipped No 83 Sqn on 3 September 1939 – the day war was declared. After a spell with Fighter Command flying Beaufighter IFs on night sorties with No 29 Sqn (during which time he claimed two victories), Gibson rejoined Bomber Command with a posting to No 106 Sqn, then equipped with Manchester Is, as its commanding officer. He was now a veteran of almost 170 operations, and held two Distinguished Service Orders (DSO) and two Distinguished Flying Crosses (DFC).

Having completed his third tour in March 1943, Gibson was posted to No 5 Group Headquarters for a period of rest on the pretext of writing a book about the bomber pilot's war. A few days later, however, he was called in to see AVM Cochrane, who asked him if he would consider forming a new squadron to undertake 'one more trip'. Gibson, who was assured that he would lead it, and also have his choice of crews, agreed.

'Squadron X', as it was initially known, began to assemble on 21 March at RAF Scampton, in Lincolnshire. At that time, the air station was home to only one unit, No 57 Sqn, leaving the base effectively at half operational strength. To oversee its creation, Flg Off (soon flight lieutenant) Harry Humphries was posted in from No 50 Sqn as adjutant, and he set about organising the several hundred air and groundcrew that were posted in, the acquisition of equipment and facilities and the myriad other duties that needed attending to. Around 26 March 'Squadron X' also gained its new identity. No 617 Sqn was officially born.

Popular myth has it that when selecting his crews, Gibson leafed through albums at No 5 Group Headquarters, selecting men personally known to him. Although he did bring three pilots from No 106 Sqn, including good friends Flt Lts John Hopgood and David Shannon, these were the exceptions. Gibson had met Flt Lt 'Mick' Martin at a

Sqn Ldr Henry 'Dinghy' Young was posted in from No 57 Sqn as No 617 Sqn's first A Flight commander. Having already survived two ditchings in the English Channel and a crash landing in North Africa prior to joining the unit, he was a highly experienced pilot and commander. Many believe that Young would have become the next squadron CO had he survived the Dams raid (*Rawson Family*)

Buckingham Palace investiture, where they had discussed low-flying techniques, and he invited him to join the unit. However, New Zealander Flt Lt Les Munro from No 97 Sqn recalled that a circular was issued by No 5 Group asking for volunteers. However, Plt Off Geoff Rice was simply told that he was being posted across from No 57 Sqn – something he was not at all pleased about.

The crews were ordered to report seven at a time, with the first group due on 24 March, the second the following day and the rest between the 26th and 31st of that month. In the event, 22 crews arrived well into the second week of April, and they were not always complete.

In the main, the principles laid down by ACM Harris were generally followed, with most of the captains being quite experienced. Indeed, some 13 of the 22 were decorated with at least one award, several having more, although their crew members were generally less experienced, with two (including Gibson's own bomb aimer) yet to fly any operations at all. The two men chosen as flight commanders were Sqn Ldrs Henry Melvyn Young and Henry Maudslay, who were given command of A and B Flights, respectively.

Young already had an eventful tour of operations behind him with No 102 Sqn, having twice been forced to ditch in the sea when returning from raids. With this, and his being a former member of the 1938 Oxford Boat Race crew, the nickname 'Dinghy' was inevitable. Young survived a further crash in January 1942 in the Middle East, before joining No 57 Sqn at Scampton in March 1943 as C Flight commander. He had made only a handful of training flights with this unit before being posted to No 617 Sqn.

Maudslay completed his first tour of 28 operations in November 1941, collecting a DFC at the end of it. After more than a year as an instructor at a conversion unit, his repeated requests for a return to operations saw him rewarded with a posting to No 50 Sqn in early March 1943.

The three principal ground officers selected were Plt Offs Henry 'Doc' Watson (Armaments), Cliff 'Capable' Caple (Engineering) and George Hodgson (Electrical). Watson had known Gibson in the early days of the war when they served together in No 83 Sqn, and by the time he joined No 617 Sqn, he had received a Mention in Dispatches (MiD) and an MBE for his work in armaments. Caple had engineering in his blood. His father had worked for Rolls-Royce, where he had designed the engine that powered the 1928 King's Cup air race winner, and both he and Watson had joined the RAF as teenage apprentices at RAF Halton.

The rest of the groundcrew were all drawn from squadrons within No 5 Group, with Flt Sgts Richard Smith and Bill Glover being given charge of A and B Flights, respectively. A third non-flying flight was also set up, known as the Repair and Maintenance (R&M) Flight, and this was commanded by Flt Sgt Albert Sansom. Despite ACM Harris' guidelines, Sansom had never worked on Lancasters before, instead coming from a Short Stirling squadron. He later recalled;

'My joining No 617 Sqn could be called a mistake, or at least contrived. As a recently promoted flight sergeant, I had been posted to RAF Syerston to replace a Flt Sgt Pike who had orders to join to No 617 Sqn. His impending loss to Syerston was not liked by the powers that be, and as I had not unpacked, it seemed reasonable to send me in his place. I duly arrived at RAF Scampton, but my lack of Lancaster experience was not the best of introductions to Plt Off Cliff Caple, who promptly made me the flight sergeant in charge of R&M Flight!'

As per orders, the other squadrons in No 5 Group each relinquished a Lancaster B I or B III to No 617 Sqn. Most were new aircraft, having taken part in no operations prior to their transfer, and they were generally ferried to Scampton by crews joining the unit. The aircraft allocated to A Flight were W4921 from No 106 Sqn, W4929 from No 61 Sqn, W4940 from No 57 Sqn, ED756 from No 44 Sqn and ED763 from No 467 Sqn. B Flight received W4926 from No 97 Sqn, ED329 from No 207 Sqn, ED437 from No 50 Sqn, ED735 from No 44 Sqn and LM309 from No 9 Sqn. After arrival, each machine was given a routine check, before being painted with the new No 617 Sqn code letters AJ. By Saturday, 27 March 1943, inspections were complete and No 617 Sqn pronounced ready to fly.

Later that same day the first training flight took place when Flt Lt Bill Astell took off in W4940/AJ-B for a low-level exercise around Leicester, Rugby and Birmingham, during which he 'photographed nine reservoirs'. Without specific details of the target, or even the weapon they were to use, crews were mostly confined to performing low-level cross-country exercises. Nevertheless, these came as an exciting release to them, as such flights were normally strictly forbidden. Les Munro recalled, 'We were told that we had to practice our low-level flying skills, first by day, then by night, and we didn't have to be told twice!'

Flights took place over a number of set routes across the length and breadth of the country, out over the sea and across to Northern Ireland, and these missions often included a bombing run over the Wainfleet Range in Lincolnshire. Weapons dropped were usually 10-lb or 20-lb smoke bombs – filled with Tetrachloride – that were aimed at canvas screens (used as markers). Pilots as well as bomb aimers executed the drops, while the gunners also carried out air-to-sea firing of their weapons.

With so much low flying going on it was inevitable that accidents would happen. Soon, tailwheels became festooned with foliage and fuselages became dented or marked by treetops.

The unsung heroes of all squadrons were the ever-faithful groundcrews. Here, four unknown stalwarts from No 617 Sqn's B Flight work on the port outer engine of Lancaster ED735/AJ-R at a Scampton dispersal a few weeks after the unit's formation in April 1943 (*Joan Bower*)

Pilots relax on the grass at RAF Scampton during a break from training in early April 1943. They are, from left to right, Plt Offs Les Knight and Geoff Rice, Flt Lt David Maltby, Wg Cdr Gibson and Flt Lts David Shannon, Mick Martin, Joe McCarthy and Les Munro (*Joan Bower*)

Flt Sgt George Johnson, (bomb aimer to Flt Lt Joe McCarthy) remembered flying along at around 40 ft, only for another Lancaster to pass *below* them, leaving McCarthy purple with rage. Low flying was one thing, but that was lunacy! These little incidents became so frequent that Gibson initiated a squadron fund into which any crew flouting the rules to the point of endangering their aircraft would have to contribute.

Complaints also flooded in from locals who thought that the aircrews were just fooling around. Section Officer (SO) Fay Gillon, a WAAF Intelligence Officer attached to No 617 Sqn, was given the task of alerting local authorities where she could in advance of such flights, but this quickly proved to be impossible as crews often decided on routes without her knowledge, while planned missions were delayed or cancelled through technical problems.

As training continued, the strengths and weaknesses of the crews began to emerge. At the end of the first week of April, Flt Sgt Ray Lovell was called in to see Gibson, as his crew had not come up to scratch. He was posted out on the 9th and replaced the following day by Plt Off Bill Divall from No 57 Sqn. On 25 April it was the turn of the appropriately name WO Lancaster. Gibson wanted to replace his navigator, but Lancaster declined, opting instead to keep the crew together and leave the unit as a whole. By that afternoon No 617 Sqn was another crew down. A number of individuals were also posted out, with Flt Lt Hopgood replacing two of his crew, and Gibson changing his bomb aimer. Although Flt Lt Shannon had brought most of his crew with him from No 106 Sqn, he duly gathered a new one once at Scampton and the former left. No 617 Sqn was at last shaping up.

Soon, the unit received more specific instructions. Wallis had been working on the best height from which to effectively drop *Upkeep*, which he calculated to be exactly 150 ft. However, the instrumentation in the Lancaster was not sensitive enough to gauge it accurately, so a device using two 'Aldis' signalling lamps was developed from an idea tried earlier in the war. One of the lamps was mounted in the front camera aperture pointing downwards, while a second was mounted just behind the bomb-bay angled forward, with both angled slightly to starboard so that they could be clearly seen from the cockpit. The two beams of light would bisect at exactly 150 ft below the aircraft, and when kept together on the surface of the water, they would enable the Lancaster crew to stay at the correct height for bomb delivery.

On 4 April, Maudslay flew W4926/AJ-Z down to the Royal Aeronautical Establishment (RAE) at Farnborough to have the device fitted, carrying out a successful trial over the sea a few days later. eturning to Scampton, he demonstrated the device to the rest of the crews in a series of runs across the aerodrome, and within days the squadron's electricians, led by Sgt Bill Cammack, had fitted it to W4921/AJ-C, W4940/AJ-B and ED756/AJ-H.

While No 617 Sqn trained, tests continued with the weapon. It was found that on almost every drop the casing broke, or was damaged to such an extent that it severely affected its run, while others simply sank straight away. Wallis realised that part of the problem lay in the dropping height, which needed to be drastically reduced. After some calculation he concluded it should be just 60 ft – incredibly low, and less than the wingspan of the Lancaster. Any lapse of concentration on the run in would spell disaster for the crews. Instructions were conveyed to No 617 Sqn, and the spotlight altimeter adjusted for the new height. Gibson promised Wallis that his boys would give it a 'damn good try'.

On 25 April Bill Astell took W4940/AJ-B for a low-level flight to Wainfleet, where he dropped 12 bombs from a height of 60 ft – the first time this lower dropping height was recorded. A number of others undertook similar flights that morning, and it was almost certainly the first day the new height was attempted, although crews continued to carry out drops from 150 ft well into May.

Another item of equipment given to No 617 Sqn at around this time to use was a synthetic night flying system known as 'Two-Stage Blue', involving removable panels of blue Perspex fitted to the inside of the cockpit canopy. These gave the impression of flying in moonlight during the day when worn in conjunction with goggles fitted with amber lenses. The system was only on trial at the time, and not yet in common use. On 3 April 'Dinghy' Young flew over to RAF Waddington in ED763/AJ-D so that the aircraft could be measured up and fitted out with the panels. He duly carried out a successful test flight eight days later after the aircraft had returned to Scampton. Three more Lancasters were fitted with the screens, including ED756/AJ-H, which had already been equipped with the optical altimeter.

MODIFIED LANCASTERS ARRIVE

At the start of the third week of April, No 617 Sqn began to receive the first of the new modified Lancasters. They were all Mk IIIs, with the designation Type 464 Provisioning – a title derived from the Vickers project number (as the weapon and associated equipment was designed by them), and the fact that the modification was temporary, in theory allowing the aircraft to be easily converted to standard at a later date.

Gone was the mid-upper turret, which was faired over, while the bomb-bay was minus its long doors, these having been replaced by shaped fairings to the front and rear. Two heavy, cast aluminium V-shaped arms had been attached to the fuselage sides below the wings, hinged at the top to allow them to move outwards. Each arm contained a large disc at the lower end, with the starboard one attached to a small

As No 617 Sqn came together at RAF Scampton, trials continued with *Upkeep* on the north Kent coast. A Type 464 Provisioning Lancaster – one of two used for trial drops – releases an *Upkeep* mine at Reculver in April 1943, clearly showing the weapon's final form

hydraulic motor located in the forward bomb-bay by means of a drive belt. There were other minor modifications too, including reworked hydraulic and oil systems, a larger bomb aimer's blister, engine improvements, a second altimeter fitted to the cockpit canopy framing and, on some aircraft, the removal of the de-icing equipment and balloon cable cutters. No two machines were identical though, as some modifications were found to be less effective than others, and these were then changed or modified on later aircraft.

The first to arrive was ED909, which was allocated to Flt Lt Mick Martin with the code AJ-P. After initial work, it was ready for him to fly on a 25-minute air test on 27 April. Finding that all was well with the new bomber, he flew it again that same day on a 50-minute 'tactical practice'.

During these training flights, the crews had found that both air-to-air and air-to-ground communication at low level was unsatisfactory when using the standard TR1154/55 wireless sets. These were subsequently replaced with smaller TR1196 units, but the improvement was minimal, so advice was sought from the RAE Radio Department, which suggested that the more reliable TR1143 set (normally used in fighters) be tried. An installation was made in ED933/AJ-X and tested on 8 May by Sqn Ldr Maudslay, who found it to be a vast improvement. At the same time Flt Lt Bob Hutchison (Gibson's wireless operator and the squadron signals leader) oversaw the construction of booths in the crew room to allow the wireless operators additional training time on the ground.

With the correct height for dropping the weapon now decided, Wallis turned his attention to determining the best distance from the dam at which to release the bomb, and how to gauge it. In the end simple trigonometry provided the answer after he calculated that the bomb should be dropped 400 to 450 yards from the dam wall. As luck would have it, both the Möhne and Eder Dams had two towers built symmetrically from the centre that could provide an 'aiming point' for the crews to use. The distance between the two towers became the base of an imaginary triangle, while the release point, up-water of the dam, was the apex.

With the known dimensions, Wallis could easily work out the required angles, which were then passed to the squadron for the bomb aimers to experiment with. Several methods based around the dimensions were tried, with the one most favoured being a hand-held wooden sight that had an eyepiece at one end and two nails at the other. Looking through the eyepiece, the bomb aimer would release the weapon when the towers on the dam lined up with the nails. The sights were made in the squadron workshops to individual requirements. A few bomb aimers tried using a cord against corresponding marks on the Perspex blister instead.

At the start of May the first *Upkeeps*, all inert examples, were delivered to Scampton. 'Doc' Watson was attached to No 5 Group in early April to gain experience in the use and handling of the weapon, and orders were issued that they were not to be touched by anyone until he returned on 1 May. A total of 56 were eventually delivered, with most remaining in their dark red oxide primer. Watson decided on his own method of marking the mines using chalk numbers and letters, leaving him alone knowing which mines were live and which were inert. He would later recall being told that the delivery of live mines to Scampton would be delayed, 'so as far as the (Armament) Section was concerned, the object was to have groundcrews not know whether we were bombing up for training or for real. We practiced loading up frequently, and eventually no one knew whether it was for real or not'.

As the modified Lancasters continued to arrive, most of the standard aircraft were returned to their former squadrons or other units, although those remaining were extensively flown. On 24 April, Maudslay suffered a tail wheel collapse in W4926/AJ-Z after a dusk training flight, while on 3 May Shannon struck a pole whilst taxiing in W4940 (now coded AJ-B 'bar', as the modified ED864 was now on strength and coded AJ-B).

With the proposed date of the operation rapidly approaching, there had still been no live test of an *Upkeep* and no practice drop made by the squadron. So, on the morning of Tuesday, 11 May, Gibson, Hopgood and Martin flew down to RAF Manston, in Kent, in ED932/AJ-G, ED925/AJ-M and ED909/AJ-P, respectively, where their aircraft were loaded with concrete-filled practice mines. They dropped these at Reculver, just along the coast, that afternoon, with Gibson noting his had a 'good run of 600 yards'. The following day several more crews flew down to Reculver to try and as Flt Lt Munro dropped his mine the rear of the aircraft was engulfed in shingle and spray as the weapon hit the water. He later remembered;

'I was probably a little too low, with the result that the fuselage was hit by the splash. It jammed the rear gunner in his turret, and he had to stay there until we reached base.'

That same day Maudslay damaged his aircraft (ED933/AJ-X) in a similar way, but more severely. Limping back to Scampton, the aircraft was declared Category AC (badly damaged) and handed over to Flt Sgt Sansom and his R&M Flight for repair. Normally, such damage would necessitate a return of the aircraft to Avro, but such was the pressing nature of the job there was no time available to return the bomber to the manufacturer. The following day the last modified Lancaster (ED937) arrived at Scampton and was allocated to Maudslay, coded AJ-Z, as a temporary replacement.

The first and only live *Upkeep* trial prior to the raid occurred on 13 May 1943, when an example was dropped 75 miles off the coast of Broadstairs, in Kent. It performed flawlessly and ran for almost 800 yards.

The following evening No 617 Sqn embarked on a final, near full-scale dress rehearsal, flying to two lakes and making a series of dummy attacks. Flt Lt David Maltby, who had taken ED906/AJ-J to Avro at Woodford for some minor repairs, arrived back too late, thereby

During practice drops by the squadron in mid May, several aircraft were damaged by water thrown up as the bombs hit the sea. On 12 May 1943 (only four days before the raid), Flt Lt Les Munro dropped his practice mine particularly low to the water, causing spray and shingle to pepper the underside of the bomber's fuselage. This in turn jammed the rear turret, trapping its occupant, and the latter could not be released until the aircraft returned to base

15

missing the exercise, while several other crews borrowed aircraft as their own were grounded for last minute work. Flt Lt Shannon flew ED934/AJ-K, leaving its regular pilot, Plt Off Vern Byers, to fly one of the standard aircraft (ED763/AJ-D), while Munro piloted ED886/AJ-O, which was the usual mount of Flt Sgt Townsend and crew – his own Lancaster was still being repaired after the Reculver incident.

A number of 'invited guests' flew with the squadron that night, including Grp Capt Whitworth, the Scampton Station Commander, who accompanied Gibson, and Sqn Ldr Malcolm Arthurton, the No 617 Sqn Medical Officer, who joined Maudslay's crew. Mick Martin had a more glamorous passenger in the form of SO Fay Gillon, who recorded details of the flight upon her return;

'A signal from the wing commander and all three of us are simultaneously creeping down the runway and gathering speed. Then the last bump and we are airborne. Gliding right down, practically in the "drink" and getting a QFE (altimeter height), dropping a smoke float to check the wind, and then a burst of firing from the wing commander's aeroplane, followed by a burst from all three of us. The voice of the wing commander coming over the VHF, "Standby Nos 2 and 3, No 1 going into attack". The formation breaking up, and we are circling above, while a Lancaster is dimly seen diving down and down out of sight, merging with the ground detail. Then a huge explosion and a flash of light. Right on target, wizard!

'Then our turn. Mick doing a big circle to get into position, grim determination on his face, and Jack (the navigator) and I with our noses glued to the Perspex. Down, down, twenty feet more, ten feet more, five feet more, steady, steady on an altitude of 60 ft and the run along the water. "Bomb gone" from Bob and then the pull up, up into the sky at full revs. The flash appearing right behind us, and yes, successful!'

As No 617 Sqn had been flying constant training exercises for the previous few weeks, resentment began to set in amongst the crews of No 57 Sqn, their neighbours at Scampton, who were continually flying operations. Inevitably, comments began to be passed until one afternoon, when it erupted in a free for all fight in the Officers' Mess. However, the reason for the endless training would soon become clear.

At 0900 hrs on Saturday, 15 May 1943, a signal was sent from the Assistant Chief of the Air Staff (Operations), AVM Norman Bottomley, to Bomber Command Headquarters, which read, 'Op CHASTISE. Immediate attack of targets "X", "Y" and "Z" approved. Execute at first available opportunity'. This simple message began a frantic 36 hours both at Scampton and at No 5 Group Headquarters at Grantham. AVM Cochrane journeyed over to Scampton to tell Whitworth that the operation would take place the following night.

With plenty to do, most aircraft were grounded for the day, with the only recorded flight being that of Vern Byers in one of the few remaining standard Lancasters at 1405 hrs. He took Flt Lt Norm Barlow with him on a bombing exercise to Wainfleet, returning to Scampton within the hour. Later that afternoon Barnes Wallis arrived to monitor the arming and loading of the mines, and to prepare for the briefing. Gibson, meanwhile, returned to Grantham with Cochrane, and together they discussed details of the operation.

At 1800 hrs, Gibson, Wallis and Whitworth adjourned to conduct an initial briefing at Whitworth's house with Young and Maudslay, Flt Lt Hopgood (who would act as deputy leader) and Flt Lt Bob Hay, the squadron bombing leader. Later, as he walked back to his office, Gibson was informed of the death of his beloved black Labrador 'Nigger'. The dog was familiar to all on No 617 Sqn, just as he had been to those serving in Gibson's previous command, No 106 Sqn, and the loss was felt deeply. As 'Nigger' had been decided as the codeword for a successful breach in the Möhne Dam, several also considered it a bad omen.

As 16 May broke, groundcrews moved out to the dispersals to prepare the aircraft, supplemented by the R&M Flight, who had realised at the eleventh hour that Maudslay's damaged ED933/AJ-X could not be made ready in time. Mines were brought from the bomb dump and loaded into the aircraft, and it was whilst doing this that near disaster occurred.

With the *Upkeep* secure under Mick Martin's aircraft, the pilot's manual release was accidentally tripped by someone in the cockpit. With a kick, the V-arms sprang apart and the mine dropped to the ground, embedding itself an inch into the tarmac. Electrician Cpl Beck Parsons recalled that 'everyone froze for a few seconds with fear of the unknown', before bodies poured out of the Lancaster and disappeared in all directions. Martin himself drove frantically to fetch 'Doc' Watson, who calmly declared that if it was going to explode, it would have already done so. Accompanying Martin back to the aircraft, Watson walked over and examined the mine, which, after being declared safe, was winched back into position.

From late morning the crews began to be briefed on their various jobs. The pilots and navigators were shown models of the three principal targets, and although the gunners and bomb aimers were not given a specific briefing at this point, many joined their fellow crewmen to run through some of the details, and to study the models themselves.

Of the 21 crews, two would not be flying on the operation, including the last to arrive – Bill Divall had hurt his knee and been grounded by the Medical Officer. Contrary to previous accounts, Flt Lt Wilson and his crew had actually been one of the first to arrive at Scampton, but illness meant that they too would not be going. This conveniently left 19 crews available that night for the 19 serviceable aircraft, but with Maudslay's damaged Lancaster still in the hanger, there was no spare in the event of a problem.

Luckily, ED825, which had been used in flight trials, was now standing idle as the latter were complete. So it was collected by a ferry crew and flown to Scampton, where the aircraft was prepared in case it was needed. The Lancaster was given the code AJ-T and fitted with several items of equipment, although not the spotlight altimeter – there was no time available to install it.

FINAL BRIEFING

At 1800 hrs all aircrew assembled for the final briefing. Gibson began by introducing Barnes Wallis, who explained exactly how *Upkeep* worked. Of the three main dams they were to attack, the Möhne and Eder were 'gravity' dams – huge curving masonry walls which held back millions of tons of water, partly by their shape. The other, the Sorpe, was an 'earth'

This official photograph shows an *Upkeep* mine under Wg Cdr Guy Gibson's Lancaster ED932/AJ-G on 20 May 1943. The aircraft was usually parked on the grass near the No 617 Sqn hanger, but on this occasion it was moved to a hardstanding to allow for a series of photographs of the weapon, and its associated equipment, to be taken (*Harry Humphries*)

dam, which had a straight, central concrete core protected on either side by sloping earth banks. If these were breached with bombs to spare, several others were listed as secondary targets.

For the attack on the Möhne and Eder, *Upkeep* was to be spun backwards before release using the small motor in the bomb-bay, which was controlled by the wireless operator. The spotlight device would be switched on by the flight engineer and monitored through the starboard cockpit window by the navigator, while the bomb aimer would be watching the target approaching in front of him, releasing the mine when at the correct distance according to the bombsight. Because of the Sorpe Dam's construction, the attack there would be slightly different. The crews were to fly along the crest, dropping their mine without spinning it, as near to the centre as they could judge.

The force was split into three waves. The main wave (Wave 1) comprised nine aircraft led by Gibson, and would include his deputy Hopgood and both flight commanders. They would take off in three groups of three and head initially for the Möhne Dam, and if successfully breached, any crew who still had a mine aboard would then head for the Eder Dam. The next group (Wave 2), which actually departed first, consisted of five aircraft taking off individually a few minutes apart. Their target was the Sorpe Dam. The last wave (Wave 3) was made up of the remaining five aircraft, which would take off individually and be diverted en route as and where they were needed. If the primary targets had yet to be breached they would be sent to supplement the main force, otherwise they would be directed to the secondary targets.

With a few more details covered, the briefing wound up, with the crews retiring to the mess to while away the next few hours. Hopgood confessed to David Shannon that he thought he would not be coming back – feelings shared by his navigator Flg Off Ken Earnshaw. Others confessed to feeling nervous or sick, but all just wanted to get underway. At 2100 hrs Flt Lt Hutchison fired a red very light into the sky, which was the pre-arranged signal for the first and second wave aircraft to start their engines. Operation *Chastise* was underway.

OPERATIONS ON

The first aircraft due to take-off was to be Flt Lt Joe McCarthy in ED915/AJ-Q, but as he started his engines he discovered a problem with the starboard outer Merlin and quickly realised that his Lancaster was going nowhere. Remembering the spare machine, he quickly ordered his crew to disembark and make for it, fearful that another crew might have similar problems and get there first. As they did so the rest of the wave left Scampton as planned, starting with Flt Lt 'Norm' Barlow in ED927/AJ-E at 2129 hrs, followed at one minute intervals by Les Munro in ED921/AJ-W, Vern Byers in ED934/AJ-K and Geoff Rice in ED936/AJ-H. By the time McCarthy had finally gotten airborne (33 minutes late at 2201 hrs), the nine aircraft of the main wave had also left. It was to be more than two hours before the third wave would start taking off, if they were needed at all.

As Wave 2 approached the islands off the Dutch coast and prepared to turn south, small pockets of flak opened up on them, hitting

A Lancaster taking off for the Dams raid during the early evening of 16 May 1943. As the aircraft is alone and the evening sky still light, it can only be from the first wave (Wave 2), which was tasked with destroying the Sorpe Dam. In fact, it is most likely the very first aircraft to leave Scampton, namely ED927/AJ-E, flown by Flt Lt 'Norm' Barlow and his crew (*Harry Humphries*)

The modified bomb-bay of Flt Lt Joe McCarthy's regular Lancaster ED915/AJ-Q *QUEENIE CHUCK CHUCK*, which developed a problem as he started up for the raid, necessitating a switch to spare aircraft ED825/AJ-T. The former was later slightly modified so as to give *Upkeep* forward spin, and it was used in this way for overland trials of the weapon. ED915 survived the war, being struck off charge in October 1946 (*Dave Rodger*)

Munro's Lancaster and putting the intercom and compass out of action. The rear turret was also disabled. The crew quickly realised that they would be useless without the ability to communicate amongst themselves, or with other aircraft, and reluctantly decided to turn for home, landing back at Scampton bitterly disappointed at 0036 hrs. A few minutes after Munro's abandonment, Geoff Rice skimmed the sea and tore off the mine. He also scooped up a large volume of water which poured back down the fuselage and out around the rear turret, almost drowning tail gunner Sgt Steve Burns in the process. He had realised too late that he was flying too low, and with their mine gone, they also turned for home, touching down 11 minutes after Munro.

As it turned out, both crews had had lucky escapes. The same could not be said for Vern Byers, who had not even crossed the Dutch coast when he too was hit by flak as his Lancaster passed over the island of Texel. The bomber crashed into the sea a little further on at 2257 hrs. The second aircraft lost was crewed by 'Norm' Barlow. After take-off, nothing further was heard from him or his crew, the Lancaster crossing the Dutch coast and turning south. It crashed a few miles east of Rees at 2350 hrs, however, after flying into an electricity pylon, its fuel tanks exploding soon after. The self-destruct fuse on the mine, which should have been armed in the air, was still 'safe', and the weapon remained intact.

Trials had shown that *Upkeep* was unlikely to explode upon impact alone, and having come down on land, the hydrostatic fuses on Barlow's weapon were useless. Within hours the Germans had a complete and intact example of an *Upkeep* mine. Barlow's rear gunner was 17-year-old Sgt Jack Liddell, the youngest flying that night, and he died along with his crewmates.

This left only McCarthy from Wave 2, and he had made up some of the deficit by the time he crossed the Dutch coast. Having avoided serious flak damage as he headed over Holland, he turned south and continued to the Sorpe Dam, his gunners shooting at the occasional searchlight and flak position along the way. During one of these minor altercations they too had a near run – a train fired upon by Sgt Ron Batson in the front turret turned out to be heavily defended, and its return fire hit the aircraft, bursting the starboard tyre.

Flt Lt Barlow's mine was captured intact after his aircraft had flown into an electricity pylon and crashed. Tests had shown that *Upkeep* would not explode on impact alone, so a self-destruct fuse was added that had to be armed in the air by the navigator. It is almost certain that Barlow's mine had yet to be armed, and so the Germans obtained a live example within hours of the mission commencing. Here, the officer (third from right) who defused the mine is explaining its workings at the German weapons examination depot near Düsseldorf (*Gerry Zwanenberg*)

McCarthy eventually reached the Sorpe at 0015 hrs otherwise unscathed, and he was surprised to see no evidence of any attack as he was unaware of the fate of the rest of the group. After a brief look, he made his first run along the dam, but the bomb aimer, Flt Sgt George Johnson, was not happy and aborted the drop. Nine more runs were made before he was finally satisfied with the line and released the mine at an estimated height of around 30 ft (as no spotlight altimeter was fitted in this spare aircraft) just past the centre of the dam. A huge explosion sent water high into the air but no breach was seen, and after circling for a few minutes they turned for home, landing back at Scampton at 0323 hrs. The only thing they could report was minor damage to the crest of the dam.

MOHNE AND EDER ATTACKS

While Wave 2 made for the Sorpe, Wave 1 headed further south, crossing the coast just north of Walcheren. Continuing across Holland and into Germany, the lead three aircraft were caught in searchlights near Dorsten and raked by flak. Several rounds hit Hopgood's aircraft and set its port outer engine alight, also leaving him and several of the crew injured. The pilot feathered the engine and they flew on. The second group of three followed the same track in almost unopposed, but the third was not so lucky. All nine Lancasters came under fire, and Bill Astell's aircraft was hit hard. The bomber flew straight into overhead power lines and crashed in flames a few miles further on. The fused mine rolled away and exploded seconds later.

The remaining eight Lancasters of the main wave arrived over the Möhne just after midnight. After Gibson had made one dummy run he turned in to make his attack and dropped his mine exactly as he had been trained to, but it veered slightly off track to the left and fell short,

A pre-war photograph of the Möhne Dam, along with the original powerhouse (the square building seen to the left of centre) that was damaged by Flt Lt John Hopgood's mine when it bounced over the dam and exploded close by. The subsequent flooding destroyed the rest of the building, which was rebuilt after the war in a different location (*Beck Parsons*)

exploding under the surface with little effect. After the waters had settled he ordered the injured Hopgood in next, but as he lined up his aircraft, the gunners on the dam quickly found their mark and he was hit again, causing the bomb aimer to drop the mine late. It bounced over the dam and landed near the power station on the other side, exploding seconds later as the self-destruct fuse detonated. As Hopgood struggled with the controls, three crew bailed out at very low level, two successfully, but seconds later the wing folded and the Lancaster crashed in flames with the remaining crew still aboard.

Mick Martin attacked next in ED909/AJ-P. To help draw the flak, Gibson flew on his starboard side, but despite this Martin's aircraft was hit in a starboard fuel tank (which was empty) and his mine also fell short, bouncing far off track to the left and exploding with no effect near the bank of the lake.

With three mines now used Gibson next ordered in 'Dinghy' Young in ED887/AJ-A, with Martin alongside, while Gibson flying around the airside of the dam to further confuse the enemy gunners. Young's mine was released and made 'three good bounces', as Gibson later recalled, before striking the dam right in the centre and sinking. After a wait of what must have seemed like hours, the mine exploded.

The crews circling waited for the waters to settle, but they could clearly see that the dam had not been breached, so David Maltby, in ED906/AJ-J, was called in next. Both Gibson and Martin flew alongside to engage the enemy gunners and draw the flak, but as Maltby approached the dam he noticed the top starting to crumble. His own bomb aimer released the mine, which struck the dam and exploded with the now customary fountain of water. As Gibson wheeled round and looked back, he could see water pouring through two breaches in the dam wall and cascading down the valley.

Barnes Wallis had predicted that a single bomb, if placed correctly, should have been enough to start a breach, with the pressure of the water doing the rest. His calculations were correct. Gibson radioed Shannon and instructed he, Maudslay, Knight (with the three remaining mines) and 'Dinghy' Young (as Deputy Leader) to follow him to the Eder Dam, about 15 minutes' flying time away. Martin and Maltby headed for home.

With time getting on, Gibson was keen to begin the attack, and he ordered Shannon in first. The latter tried three times to align his mine with the dam but met with little success, so he was instructed to hold off to allow Maudslay (in ED937/AJ-Z) to have a go. He experienced similar problems to Shannon, and after two runs also failed to release his mine.

The approach to the Eder was far more difficult than at the Möhne, necessitating a drop from 1000 ft down to the water, before turning sharply to port and dipping down over a spit of land. Shannon tried again, making two more runs before dropping his mine on the third. It bounced twice prior to hitting the dam wall and exploding, but no breach was seen. Maudslay then tried again, but his mine dropped late, striking the crest of the dam and exploding just after the aircraft had passed over the target. Gibson called Maudslay over the radio, and received a reply that he was 'Okay', but nothing more was heard from the crew.

This photograph of the Eder Dam was taken during the late morning of 17 May 1943, and it clearly shows the breach caused by the mine from Plt Off Les Knight's aircraft (*Beck Parsons*)

With his aircraft badly damaged by the explosion, Maudslay immediately tried to make his way home. However, approaching Emmerich, on the German/Dutch border, some 90 minutes later, the Lancaster came under fire from flak batteries on the edge of the town and crashed in a field seconds later. There were no survivors.

Back at the Eder Dam, the destruction of the target now rested squarely on the shoulders of Plt Off Les Knight and his crew. He too found the approach hard, and had already made one abortive attempt before circling around for a second try. His mine bounced three times and hit the wall just off-centre. As they circled round, water could clearly be seen pouring through a wide breach. The four aircraft turned for home.

For most, the return flight was largely uneventful, but as 'Dinghy' Young approached the Dutch coast near Ijmuiden flak guns opened up on his aircraft, inflicting damage that set a wing on fire. Moments later the Lancaster crashed into the sea in flames.

THE MOBILE RESERVE

About 20 minutes before Gibson had begun his attack on the Möhne, the first aircraft of the mobile reserve, ED910/AJ-C, flown by Plt Off 'Bill' Ottley, took off. He was followed two minutes later at 0011 hrs by Plt Off 'Lew' Burpee in ED865/AJ-S, then Flt Sgt Ken Brown in ED918/AJ-F at 0012 hrs, Flt Sgt Bill Townsend in ED886/AJ-O at 0014 hrs and, finally, Flt Sgt Cyril Anderson in ED924/AJ-Y at 0015 hrs.

Having received confirmation that both the Möhne and Eder Dams had been breached, No 5 Group radioed Brown at 0224 hrs and diverted him to the Sorpe, which he found a short time later shrouded in heavy mist. After several unsuccessful runs, he instructed his wireless operator, Sgt Harry Hewstone, to drop flares to help mark a path, before bringing the Lancaster around again for his tenth run. Brown flew along the crest of the dam and dropped his mine about two-thirds of the way across, but no breach was seen, and with no more aircraft in the vicinity, they turned for home, landing back at Scampton at 0533 hrs.

Four minutes after contacting Brown, No 5 Group radioed Ottley to divert him to the Lister Dam – one of the secondary targets – which the crew acknowledged. However, a message sent immediately after re-diverting them to the Sorpe was met with only silence, as did another 20 minutes later.

At that very moment Ottley was bathed in searchlight and under fire, which set the port inner engine ablaze. Struggling to stay in the air, he shouted over the intercom, 'I'm sorry boys we've had it' as the aircraft began to break up. One of the wing fuel tanks exploded, and the Lancaster hit the ground on the edge of a wood a few miles from Hamm, the mine exploding seconds later. By some miracle the rear turret broke off, throwing out the rear gunner Flt Sgt Fred Tees, who, regaining his composure some time later, staggered to a nearby farmhouse. Here he remained until the police arrived to take him into custody. Tees was the only survivor of the Ottley crew.

No 5 Group next attempted to call Burpee to divert him to the Sorpe, but he and his crew were already dead by then. They had strayed slightly from the briefed route and close to the Luftwaffe base at Gilze-Rijen, where the bomber had come under intense flak and been hit. The aircraft crashed in flames on the edge of the airfield at 0200 hrs, with the fused mine exploding minutes later, destroying and damaging dozens of airfield buildings.

This left just two Lancasters in the wave with their mines intact. At 0222 hrs, No 5 Group called Townsend, and ordered him to the Enneppe Dam (another of the secondary targets), which they reached about 50 minutes later. The crew made three runs over the dam before dropping their mine on the fourth, but it fell short and exploded without effect in the centre of the reservoir. On the way home they encountered a few pockets of flak, but landed safely back at Scampton at 0615 hrs. Townsend's crew was the last to make it home.

At the same time that Townsend was trying to locate his target, Anderson was on his way home. He had been forced off track by searchlights and flak north of the Ruhr, and then found a problem with the rear turret. Diverted to the Sorpe at 0228 hrs, the crew pondered their position. With dawn approaching, and being slightly lost, they instead decided to turn for home, landing back at Scampton at 0530 hrs with their mine still aboard.

Considering that the Sorpe Dam remained intact, and that so many were lost, Anderson's decision was condemned by many of those who had returned. Gibson was furious, later telling Joe McCarthy that the crew had simply 'flown up and down the North Sea for the full time'. The following day, after some group photographs were taken, Anderson and his crew 'were put on a train back to No 49 Sqn a few hours later, and no word was ever mentioned of them again'.

Some of the surviving Dams raid aircrew were photographed on the steps of the Officers' Mess at RAF Scampton the day after the raid. They are, in the back row, from left to right, Sgt Townsend (pilot), Plt Off Howard (navigator), Flt Lt McCarthy (pilot), Flt Lt Wilson (pilot), Flt Lt Munro (pilot), Wg Cdr Gibson (pilot), Plt Off Fort (bomb aimer), Flg Off Hobday (navigator), Flt Lt Maltby (pilot), Flg Off Johnson (bomb aimer), Flg Off Taerum (navigator), Plt Off Spafford (bomb aimer) and Flt Lt Trevor-Roper (rear gunner). And front row, from left to right, Sgt Anderson (pilot), Flt Lt Hutchison (wireless operator), Plt Off Rice (pilot), Flt Lt Martin (pilot), Flt Lt Shannon (pilot) Plt Off Buckley (rear gunner), Plt Off Knight (pilot) and Flg Off Chambers (wireless operator) (*Joan Bower*)

Having been debriefed, the crews adjourned to their messes too excited to sleep. As the following morning dawned, there was a party atmosphere around Scampton. Eight crews had failed to return, including both flight commanders and the deputy leader, but despite this, the long hours of intense training had been vindicated with two dams breached and a third (the Sorpe) damaged. All flying personnel were stood down with immediate effect, the groundcrews receiving three days' leave and the aircrews seven. Within days the announcement of awards was made – a Victoria Cross (VC) to Gibson, two Conspicuous Gallantry Medals to other pilots and 31 other awards. Several groundcrew also received commendations.

Ten days later, the King and Queen visited Scampton during a tour of Lincolnshire airfields. After lunch in the Officers' Mess, they toured various areas of the station and inspected air and groundcrews out on the airfield. A competition had been held amongst all ranks of No 617 Sqn to design a new unit badge, and the choice had been narrowed down to two, which were now presented to the King for him to choose his preference. The first, designed by Cpl Vic Grey (one of the B Flight fitters), depicted a pair of manacled hands with the chain about to be broken by a large hammer, above the legend *'Alter the Map'*. The King, however, favoured one showing a dam broken by three bolts of

His Majesty King George VI talks to No 617 Sqn's three principal technical officers during the Royal visit to RAF Scampton on 27 May 1943 under the nose of Gibson's Lancaster ED932/AJ-G. From left to right, they are Flt Lt Cliff 'Capable' Caple (engineering officer), Flt Lt Henry 'Doc' Watson (armament officer) and Plt Off James Hodgson (electrical officer) (*Beck Parsons*)

After inspecting the air- and groundcrews, the Royal party moved to the No 617 Sqn hangar and crew room, where the King (third from left) was asked to choose a design for a new unit badge, designs for which had been the result of a squadron competition. Also shown (from left) are AVM Cochrane (No 5 Group C-in-C), Wg Cdr Gibson and Grp Capt Whitworth (commander RAF Scampton) (*Beck Parsons*)

Aircrew of No 617 Sqn pose outside Buckingham Palace after their investiture on 22 June 1943, where they were presented with their awards by Queen Elizabeth. Wg Cdr Gibson, who received the VC, stands in the centre, with his head turned to the left (*Malcolm Arthurton*)

lightning, over the motto *'Apres Moi Le Deluge'* ('After Me The Flood'), and this was subsequently sent to the Chester Herald for his approval.

Those who had been awarded medals travelled down to London in late June, accompanied by several others from the squadron, to receive them at a Buckingham Palace Investiture on the 22nd. Outside, the newsreel cameras rolled and dozens of formal and informal photographs were taken, with many appearing in the papers over the following days. Once recognised, few had to pay for drinks or taxis.

BACK TO REALITY, AND OPERATIONS

As no firm decision had yet been taken as to No 617 Sqn's long-term future, or role, the first duty was to bring in new crews to replace those who had been lost. Flt Lt Ralph Allsebrook had arrived a few days after the raid, with Flg Off 'Cab' Kellaway following at the end of June. On 2 July Plt Off 'Bunny' Clayton and Sqn Ldr George Holden joined the unit, the latter taking command of B Flight, while David Maltby, promoted to squadron leader the day after the Dams raid, took over A Flight. As the weeks went on No 617 Sqn settled back into the routine of training flights, leave and other duties, while its future was discussed.

Back in February 1943 when the use of *Upkeep* was first being considered, numerous other targets were looked at, including dock installations, U- and E-boat pens and canals. In the case of the latter, Wallis envisaged dropping the mine on land for it to 'bounce' forward, before dropping into the water and exploding, breaching the banks and flooding the surrounding area. At the start of June, Lancasters' ED915 and ED932 were flown down to RAE Farnborough to have the small motor in their bomb-bay altered to give *Upkeep* forward rather than backward spin, which it was hoped would increase its range over land. Trials began a few days later at the Ashley Walk bombing range in Hampshire.

No 617 Sqn, meanwhile, continued training in 'Dambuster' techniques, much of the latter consisting of low-flying exercises along the same routes used for the Dams raid. They also began to re-equip with standard Lancasters, and these exercises were carried out with a

The first replacement crew to join No 617 Sqn was that of Flt Lt Ralph Allsebrook, who was posted in three days after the Dams raid. Pictured in late April 1943 just before they left No 49 Sqn are, from left to right, Flg Off Grant (wireless operator), Flt Sgt Lulham (bomb aimer), Flt Lt Allsebrook (pilot), Plt Off Botting (navigator), Sgt Hitchen (mid-upper gunner), Flt Sgt Moore (flight engineer) and Sgt Jones (rear gunner) (*Tomos Roberts*)

mixture of both aircraft. By mid-July though, boredom had begun to settle back in amongst the crews, and several were becoming restless at the continued inactivity. With the long training period before the Dams raid too, most had flown just a single combat operation in the previous three-and-a-half months.

At the end of the second week of July, therefore, No 617 Sqn was detailed for only its second operation – a bombing raid to northern Italy. Even with the new aircraft, the squadron was still not at full strength, and so it borrowed several Lancasters from neighbouring No 57 Sqn.

Taking off on 15 July, the 12 aircraft were split into two groups of six, with the first of these, led by Holden, attacking the electricity sub-station at Aquata Scrivia. Although the target became engulfed in smoke, several

Sqn Ldr David Maltby poses with his crew at RAF Blida after the raid on San Polo D'Enza on 15 July 1943. Maltby had deputised for Wg Cdr Gibson after the Dams raid, and was a popular member of the squadron. He was ultimately overlooked as No 617 Sqn's new commander when Gibson left, however, the job instead going to Sqn Ldr George Holden. These men are, from left to right, Sgt Vic Hill (mid upper gunner), Sgt Anthony Stone (wireless operator), Plt Off John Fort (bomb aimer), Sqn Ldr David Maltby (pilot), Sgt Bill Hatton (flight engineer) and Sgt Harold Simmonds (rear gunner), while Sgt Viv Nicholson (navigator) is kneeling in front of the group (*Grace Blackburn*)

The starboard wheel of Les Munro's Lancaster EE150/AJ-Z, which burst as he landed at RAF Blida after the operation to San Polo D'Enza on 15 July 1943. Thankfully no one was injured, and the bomber was quickly repaired, allowing the crew to return to the UK on 24 July with the rest of the squadron (*Greg Pigeon*)

When No 617 Sqn targeted the power station at San Polo D'Enza on 15 July 1943, it was still not fully equipped with standard Lancasters. Numbers had to be made up through the borrowing of several aircraft from other units, therefore, including W5008/DX-B from No 57 Sqn – it was was flown on the operation by Plt Off Geoff Rice. The aircraft is seen here taking off on a brief air test from RAF Blida, prior to undertaking the return flight to the UK on 24 July (*Alex Maynard*)

crews obtained direct hits, with Plt Off Townsend (newly commissioned) also hitting an ammunition train, which exploded with spectacular results. Ken Brown could not positively locate the target and instead diverted to bomb Genoa, while the other six aircraft, led by David Maltby, attacked the sub-station at San Polo d'Enza, although they too had some difficulty locating the target because of haze. However, good results were reported and the operation was considered a moderate success.

After bombing, all crews flew on to RAF Blida, in Algeria, where they were due to stay for a few days before returning to the UK. As it turned out, bad weather delayed the flight by almost a week – something not unwelcome by the crews, who could bask in the warm North African weather, eat fresh fruit and swim during their stay. As the weather cleared, and they prepared to return home, they were briefed to bomb the docks at Leghorn, a port city on the western edge of Tuscany, on the way.

Leaving Blida on 24 July, the Lamcasters set course for the target, although they again found it obscured by haze. Despite this, McCarthy reported hitting an oil dump and Munro a railway yard. Allsebrook had a more eventful flight than the rest when he lost his starboard outer propeller after its shaft fractured. He pressed on with three engines, arriving late and making two runs, before releasing his bombs on an oil dump. He eventually arrived back at Scampton after midnight on 25 July, having by then been in the air for more than nine hours.

Before leaving Blida, crews took the opportunity to load up with wine, fresh fruit and other luxuries. Sgt Bill Morris, serving at Blida with the 2nd Air Formation Signals, recalled how the aircraft also took packages home for those on the base. 'My parents were amazed to receive the basket of fruit postmarked Norwich when they knew I was in North Africa!'

Sgt Tom Maynard, mid-upper gunner to Plt Off Geoff Rice, talks to some local goatherds during No 617 Sqn's brief stay at RAF Blida in July 1943. Maynard was killed, along with five of his crew, on 20 December 1943 during an operation to Liege, only Geoff Rice surviving (*Alex Maynard*)

No 617 Sqn ended July with another operation, this time dropping leaflets over northern Italy on the 29th. Known as 'nickels', these trips were unpopular, as they were seen as having little worth despite carrying the same risk as a normal bombing mission. McCarthy and Shannon were detailed to drop theirs over Bologna, Maltby, Kellaway and Divall over Milan, Holden and Munro over Genoa and Knight and Rice over Turin. Again, they were hampered by haze, so much so that McCarthy headed for Milan instead.

One highlight of the operation though was a return to Blida, and this time they had taken some provisions out. Morris again recalled, 'They brought out small barrels of good old English beer. We were most grateful'. Seven of the nine crews returned to Scampton on 1 August (without bombing any targets on the way), although McCarthy and Munro were delayed (much to their delight!) for minor servicing to their aircraft. After a short stop at Ras-el Ma, in Morocco, on the way back, McCarthy arrived at Scampton on 5 August and Munro three days later.

A NEW COMMANDER

Although No 617 Sqn had now undertaken three operations since the Dams raid, Guy Gibson had not flown with them. When asked to form the squadron by the No 5 Group commander, it was to fly just 'one more trip', and Cochrane stuck to his word. Thereafter, Gibson had been called upon to undertake numerous official and celebrity duties.

Unknown to the unit at the time, Gibson took off with his crew and the B Flight commander George Holden in ED933/AJ-X on 2 August for what would be his last flight with No 617 Sqn – a low-level cross-country hop lasting 1 hour and 25 minutes. After landing, Gibson gathered his crew and groundcrew, and with Holden, was photographed next to ED932/AJ-G by the station photographic section in an informal 'hand-over'. The next day he departed for London and thence to North America on a tour, passing his crew and command of No 617 Sqn to Holden.

From the point of view of operational experience and awards, Sqn Ldr George Walton Holden could match the most experienced pilots

The informal hand over of No 617 Sqn by Wg Cdr Gibson to Sqn Ldr Holden after a brief training flight on 2 August 1943. Gibson assembled his air- and groundcrew next to ED932/ AJ-G and had the moment captured on film by the RAF Scampton Photographic Section. He ordered 12 copy prints to be made up, which he then signed on the front. After the rest of the crew had signed the reverse, he presented a copy to each of those featured. Gibson then had the negative destroyed. The personnel in this photograph are, from left to right, LACs Ray Harding and Frank Twigg, Plt Off Jim Deering, unknown, Flt Lts Richard Trevor-Roper and Bob Hutchison, Wg Cdr Guy Gibson, Cpl Derek Wood, Sqn Ldr George Holden, Sgt John Elliot, Plt Off Fred Spafford and LAC Roy Vivian (*Colin Hutchison*)

Plt Off Bill Divall, his navigator Plt Off Doug Warwick and Flt Lt Bob Hutchison at RAF Blida in July 1943. Divall and Warwick had missed the Dams raid, much to their bitter disappointment, after Divall injured his knee. Bob Hutchison flew as wireless operator to Wg Cdr Gibson and was the squadron Signals Leader, before crewing up with Sqn Ldr George Holden after the Dams raid (*Doug Warwick*)

on No 617 Sqn. He had completed a first tour of 32 operations on Whitleys and Halifaxs with Nos 78 and 35 Sqns, respectively, between October 1940 and August 1941, and after a period of test flying and instruction (where he completed another two operations), had begun a second tour as commanding officer of No 102 Sqn in October 1942. Holden, who completed a further 11 trips before his posting to No 617 Sqn came through, was the holder of a DSO and two DFCs.

However, he proved to be unpopular amongst many of the crews, who remember him as something of a show-off – 'too flash' – and occasionally arrogant. Whilst at Blida after the first July raid, he saw a local goat herder with his flock wandering on the edge of the airfield and drove a jeep straight at them in a show of bravado – a display deemed deeply distasteful by those watching. Holden's flight engineer, Sgt John Pulford, revealed his own dislike of the man during a conversation with a friend, which probably explains why he did not accompany Holden on the return leg back to Scampton. Holden seemingly flew without an engineer, while Pulford came back with Ken Brown. On the 29 July raid, Holden had again flown without Pulford, instead borrowing 'Bunny' Clayton's engineer. The two men did not fly together again.

Continuing the overland *Upkeep* trials, on 4 August five crews flew down to Ashley Walk bombing range, where Barnes Wallis watched them from the ground. Although one weapon failed to release, four dropped successfully and performed well, running about 1100 yards before reaching the target. The following day five more aircraft flew down to Ashley Walk, this time dropping against solid concrete structures instead of the canvas screens used the previous day.

'Cab' Kellaway, in ED765/AJ-M, was the last to make his run, but as he did so he caught the slipstream of the proceeding aircraft, which made the Lancaster difficult to control. Immediately faced with a row of pylons, he tried to fly under them, but the port wingtip hit the ground and the aircraft crashed nose first, sliding across the ground before catching fire. Kellaway received a broken leg while the bomb aimer, Flt

In October 1942 Wg Cdr George Holden became the commanding officer of No 102 Squadron at RAF Pocklington. He had already flown 34 operations, all on Halifaxs, and completed another 11 with the unit prior to joining No 617 Sqn on 2 July 1943 as its B Flight commander. Having dropped to squadron leader in order to fill this position, Holden became No 617 Sqn's next CO on 2 August, but was killed on its next operation, to the Dortmund-Ems Canal, on 15 September 1943

Sgt Bill Harris, was thrown out of the aircraft. He was found later, lying between the two starboard engines with serious head injuries. In the event, Harris never flew on operations again, but the rest escaped with only bruises and other minor injuries. ED765 had been the first 'Dambuster' Lancaster to be modified, and was used in trials with the mine before being flown to Scampton for use by No 617 Sqn on 8 July.

Despite the trials being deemed satisfactory, it was decided not to use *Upkeep* over land, although thoughts of employing the mine against other water-related targets persisted. The squadron continued to practice high and low-level flying over land and sea, and continued with practise drops (using smoke bombs) at the Wainfleet Bombing Range.

At the end of August No 617 Sqn received notice that it was to move home, departing RAF Scampton for a new base at RAF Coningsby on the 30th. The latter was better suited to heavy bomber operations, having a concrete runway, whereas Scampton retained grass (although it was now planned to lay concrete). Most of the groundcrews were flown over on squadron aircraft, and by that evening some sections were operating as normal. By the end of the following day, No 617 Sqn was reported to be 'functioning more or less normally'.

Around the same time as this move, the unit was allocated new squadron codes. Although the exact date of the switch has never been confirmed, it almost certainly coincided with the base move. While the 14 remaining 'Dambuster' Lancasters (including those originally used in trials but now also on strength with No 617 Sqn) retained the AJ coding, the standard aircraft were marked with the letters KC.

While discussion on the future of the unit, and the mounting of further Dambuster raids, continued on high, No 617 Sqn was detailed for another operation on 14 September, this time against the heavily defended Dortmund-Ems Canal. This was a vitally important waterway, which despite being subjected to repeated attacks since mid 1940 was still in constant use. As the plan to use *Upkeep* against canals had been dropped, squadron aircraft would instead be carrying another new weapon – a single 12,000-lb High Capacity (HC) bomb each, known as a 'blockbuster'.

Eight aircraft, led by Holden, left Coningsby, accompanied by six Mosquitos from Nos 605 and 418 Sqns as fighter cover, but at 0038 hrs, while still over the North Sea, No 5 Group sent a recall signal as the weather had severely deteriorated over the target. As they turned for home, Maltby's JA981/KC-J was seen to hit the sea and explode, and although Shannon circled the area for over two hours until an Air-Sea Rescue (ASR) launch reached the area, nothing was seen of the aircraft or crew.

The exact reason for Maltby's loss has never been determined. There have been suggestions that he might have misjudged

A 12,000lb HC 'Blockbuster' bomb is dropped over the Ashley Walk bombing range during a trial by the A&EE in April 1944. No 617 Sqn first used this weapon on the disastrous Dortmund-Ems Canal operation on 15 September 1943 (*Paul Clark*)

his height or caught the slipstream of another aircraft, although with his experience both are unlikely. A further, perhaps more credible, explanation is that he was struck by an aircraft from another squadron returning from operations.

Indeed, a Mosquito of No 139 Sqn (DZ598/XD-N) was lost during a raid on Berlin that same night. Nothing further was heard from it after take-off, so it cannot be confirmed how far the crew got, but certainly the return route for the No 139 Sqn crews that night crossed the outbound one of No 617 Sqn, and the timings are close. Whatever the reason, only David Maltby's body was recovered, found the following morning by another ASR launch. The remaining seven members of his crew (including an extra gunner they were carrying that night) were not seen again.

The following night the squadron tried again. With the six Mosquitos accompanying them once more, the same eight crews set off, but this time with the addition of Mick Martin in EE150/KC-Z taking Maltby's place. After crossing the border into Germany, they were cloaked by a heavy fog that 'came down like a wall', as Martin recalled later. Further on they were engaged by light flak, which caught Holden's aircraft in the starboard inner petrol tank, setting it on fire. Flames streamed back until it exploded, the Lancaster half-turning before diving straight down and crashing onto a farm. A few minutes later the fuel, and then the bomb, went up, flattening the farmhouse and killing one of the occupants.

On board Holden's aircraft that night were four of the crew that had flown with Guy Gibson to the dams, as well as Sgt 'Sandy' Powell who had been Bill Townsend's flight engineer on the same operation. It was also George Holden's 30th birthday.

With the loss of Holden, Martin assumed control of the lead group, instructing Wilson and Knight to formate on his port and starboard side, respectively. They came under fire again near Rheims, but reached the target area without further loss and began flying box circuits, each awaiting their turn to bomb – if they could get sight of the target. Almost immediately Knight's rear gunner saw Wilson's aircraft take a direct hit by flak that started a fire. It went down, clipping some trees before crashing in a field by the canal. Fifteen minutes later the 12,000-lb bomb exploded in a huge fireball, leaving a crater ten metres wide.

Les Knight's Lancaster JB144/KC-N is about to be loaded with a 12,000-lb 'Blockbuster' at RAF Coningsby on 15 September 1943. After his aircraft was hit by flak, Knight kept it flying long enough for his crew to escape to safety, before being fatally injured when the bomber crashed. The 'DX' letters painted on the trolley indicates that it had been borrowed from No 57 Sqn, which was allocated this code in June 1940 (*Beck Parsons*)

Most of the aircraft was found the next day on the near side canal, although the rear turret, still containing the body of Sgt Eric Hornby, was found on the far bank.

The same fate almost befell Knight only minutes later. Flying too low, he hit some trees, putting two engines out of action and causing him to drop out of formation. Almost ten minutes passed before Knight came back over the radio to ask 'I have lost two engines. May I have permission to jettison, Sir?' It has been written that Martin shouted back an almost desperate 'For God's sake Les, get rid of it', but the official report compiled at debriefing notes that Martin simply replied 'Okay. Jettison. Good luck' – sentiments that were echoed by the other crews. After a few minutes of silence, Knight radioed again, 'I have successfully jettisoned and am endeavouring to return to base'. That was the last the squadron heard from him.

Flying at a height of little more than 50 ft, Knight fought to keep the Lancaster in the air, but despite the crew jettisoning every available item to reduce weight, he quickly realised the situation was hopeless. Ordering them to bail out, Knight wrestled with the controls, allowing the others time to escape, but as the last left, the aircraft turned over and crashed into a field with the pilot still aboard.

Martin, meanwhile, continued to circle the target, anxiously trying to find a break in the murk that would allow him to see the aiming point. He eventually dropped his bomb on the 13th run, having spent an incredible 84 minutes over the canal.

By this time the second flight had arrived, led by Allsebrook. He went in to attack, but dropped his bomb some way from the aiming point, before running into heavy flak from guns based next to the canal. Martin called him over the radio, and received the terse reply, 'Hang on until I get out of this', followed a few moments later by 'returning to base', but after that only silence. More flak had hit his Lancaster, and soon after a

The sad remains of JB144/KC-N in Holland the following morning. Les Knight's body is seen here being loaded into a horse-drawn hearse by Dutch locals in a photograph taken in secret, as the Germans did not permit such images to be taken by civilians. He was laid to rest in the local cemetery at Den Hamm. For sacrificing his own life in order to save those of his crew, Knight was awarded a posthumous Mention in Dispatches (*John Knight*)

wing disintegrated and the bomber clipped a house and a canal-side crane, before crashing into the water. The 12,000-lb bomb from Allsebrook's aircraft failed to explode and was recovered intact the following day by a German bomb disposal team, who quickly made detailed drawings of the weapon just as they had with *Upkeep* after the Dams raid. For the second time, an example of a new weapon had been recovered intact for examination after only its first use.

Plt Off Geoff Rice stayed in the area for almost an hour trying to identify the target through the fog, all the time attracting flak that holed his aircraft in several plaecs. Finally giving up, he turned for home, unaccountably jettisoning his bomb as he crossed back over the coast. Bill Divall also searched for the target for some time, but he too eventually fell victim to the flak, which hit the aircraft in the fuel tanks and fuselage. With the aircraft on fire, Divall ordered his bomb aimer to jettison the weapon and it fell away into the canal only moments before their Lancaster's fuel tanks exploded and they crashed on the bank of the canal. The bodies of the crew were recovered the next day, with that of the rear gunner, Sgt Daniel Allatson (who had flown as a late replacement in Ken Brown's crew on the Dams raid), still in his turret.

This left only one more aircraft still to bomb – that of David Shannon. He circled the target for 45 minutes before managing to get a quick sight of the target, whereupon he wheeled in and released his bomb, the latter on the towpath next to the canal. A few feet to one side and the canal might have been breached, but it remained intact. While the escorting Mosquitos all returned safely, having seen no fighter activity at all, No 617 Sqn paid a heavy price, with only three of the eight aircraft that had set out making it back to Coningsby.

The Dortmund-Ems operation was a total disaster, for the target remained largely undamaged and two-thirds of the crews sent to attack it had been lost. After only a handful of operations (and the aborted attempt to fly to the canal the night before), No 617 Sqn had lost its CO, four flight commanders and eight other crews. It was no surprise, therefore, that the unit quickly gained the reputation of being a 'suicide squadron'.

Martin was the last to return from the operation, and he was met by Cochrane (C-in-C No 5 Group) who had wanted to promote him to acting wing commander to assume control of No 617 Sqn. However, he was advised by Grp Capt 'Sam' Patch, the Station Commander at RAF Coningsby, that two jumps up the promotion ladder might be a little too much in one go, and after some thought Cochrane reluctantly agreed. Instead, he promoted Martin one step to squadron leader, and gave him temporary command.

One can only imagine Martin's feelings as he was taken aside and told the news, with the adrenalin of the operation still running through him, tempered by news of the losses. Martin, however, was more concerned with the failure of the operation, and told Cochrane that he was prepared to give it another crack the following night. But Cochrane resisted, as another target had already been prepared for the unit.

The Antheor Viaduct lay near Cannes, in southern France, and it carried a main rail line from Marseille to Genoa across its nine arches. Allied Intelligence estimated that thousands of tons of supplies travelled over it daily to Italy, but despite this the defences on and around the

Following the loss of George Holden on the disastrous Dortmund-Ems Canal raid, temporary command of No 617 Sqn passed to Flt Lt 'Mick' Martin, who also received a promotion to squadron leader. An Australian in the RAF, Martin was a popular member of the unit, an enthusiastic pilot and an expert at low flying. He remained in the RAF after the war, rising to the rank of air marshal in 1970, before retiring four years later (*Lady Wendy Martin*)

viaduct were fairly light. The day after the Dortmund-Ems raid, six crews, including those led by the recently commissioned Ken Brown and new arrival Flt Lt David Wilson (who was posted in on 27 August), were detailed to attack it. They were to be accompanied by six aircraft from No 619 Sqn, based at nearby Woodhall Spa, whose commanding officer, Wg Cdr 'Bill' Abercromby, would be leading the operation.

The outward flight was uneventful, although 'Bunny' Clayton experienced severe icing and returned to base early. The remaining aircraft reached the target and bombed, some from as low as 350 ft, but despite several close hits the viaduct was left largely undamaged. The Lancaster crews returned to base disappointed and frustrated at their lack of success, but at least they had suffered no losses.

A PERIOD OF REST

Having experienced fearful losses in a short space of time, the surviving crews from No 617 Sqn got the chance to take stock in September-October 1943 as the unit enjoyed an extended period off operations. Plt Off Bill Townsend and most of his crew were posted out as 'tour expired' on 17 September, while several others were posted in. However, as the low-level exercises continued, so did the accidents.

On 9 October, whilst flying in Townsend's 'Dambuster' ED886/AJ-O, WO George 'Chuffy' Bull struck the top of a tree whilst checking a map. Pulling up too late, the Perspex blister at the front of the aircraft took the brunt of the damage and shattered, injuring the bomb aimer in the head and sending a howling wind down the aircraft, along with all his maps. They returned to base immediately, where the damage was officially classified Category AC (repair beyond unit capability – may be repaired on site by another unit or contractor). After investigation the accident was put down to Bull's 'over-keeness'.

On 1 October Martin received a letter from the Chester Herald, John Heaton-Armstrong, regarding the motto 'Apres Moi Le Deluge' ('After Me The Deluge') that had been chosen for the No 617 Sqn badge. He had previously written to the office that dealt with such matters, and was told that the original seemed 'most egotistical' and 'all wrong'. The office in turn suggested that perhaps it should be changed to 'Apres Nous Le Deluge' ('After Us The Deluge'), 'as the Commanding Officer would be the last to take the credit of the job entirely upon himself'.

In his letter, Heaton-Armstrong replied that 'Apres Nous Le Deluge' had been attributed to many people, not least Madame Pompadour after the Battle of Rossbach, which was not a particularly pleasant association. He had put this to No 617 Sqn in June, although at the time their reply had been, 'As far as the motto is concerned I think it would be better to have "Apres Moi Le Deluge". Heaton-Armstrong persisted, citing many historical uses of both quotes, and in the 1 October letter he again asked if Martin would prefer 'nous'.

Martin replied on 21 October, stating that the former commanding officer and squadron crews, many of whom had subsequently laid down their lives on operations, had approved the original motto, and as their Majesties had both been 'rather attracted' by its aptness, he preferred that it remained unchanged. Unaware that the King had already given his verbal approval, Heaton-Armstrong said nothing more.

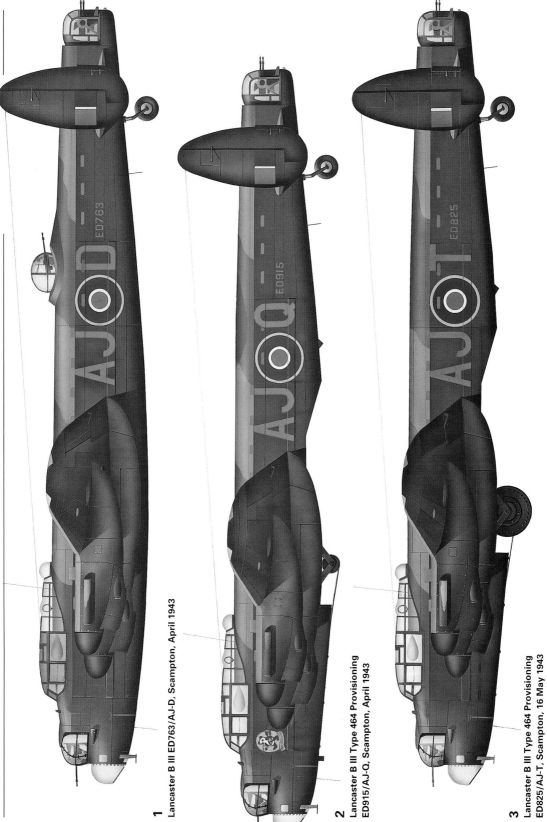

1
Lancaster B III ED763/AJ-D, Scampton, April 1943

2
Lancaster B III Type 464 Provisioning
ED915/AJ-Q, Scampton, April 1943

3
Lancaster B III Type 464 Provisioning
ED825/AJ-T, Scampton, 16 May 1943

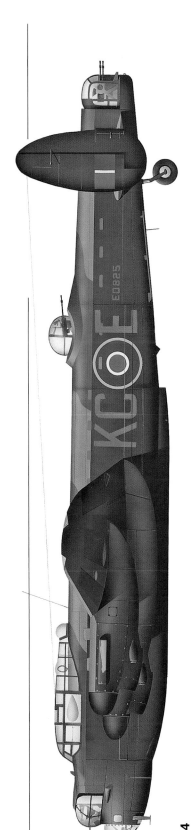

4

Lancaster B III Type 464 Provisioning ED825 KC-E, Tempsford, 10 December 1943

5

Lancaster B III Type 464 Provisioning ED912/KC-S, Coningsby, December 1943

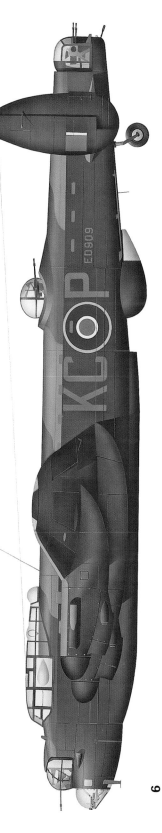

6

Lancaster B III Type 464 Provisioning ED909/KC-P, Woodhall Spa, 8 June 1944

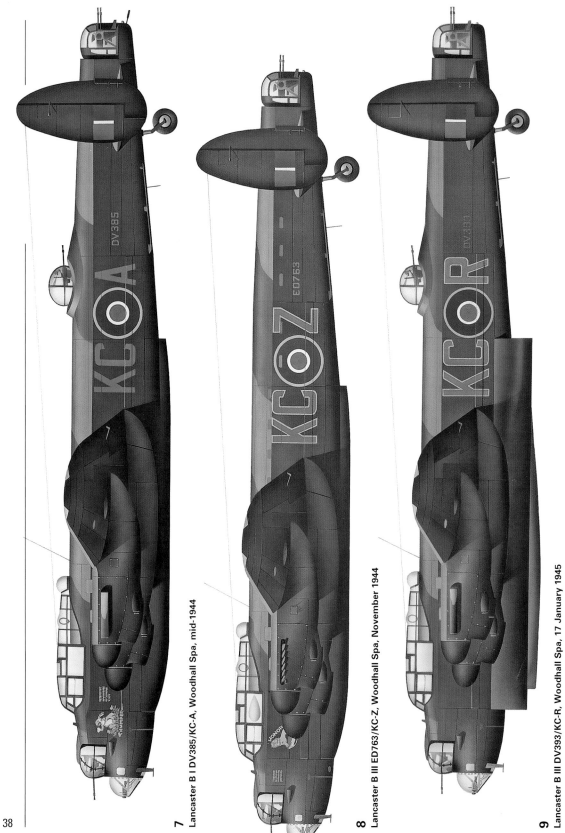

7

Lancaster B I DV385/KC-A, Woodhall Spa, mid-1944

8

Lancaster B III ED763/KC-Z, Woodhall Spa, November 1944

9

Lancaster B III DV393/KC-R, Woodhall Spa, 17 January 1945

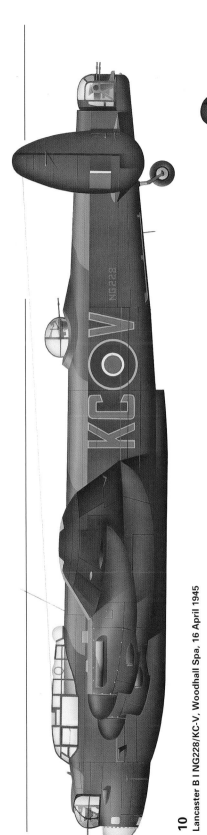

10
Lancaster B I NG228/KC-V, Woodhall Spa, 16 April 1945

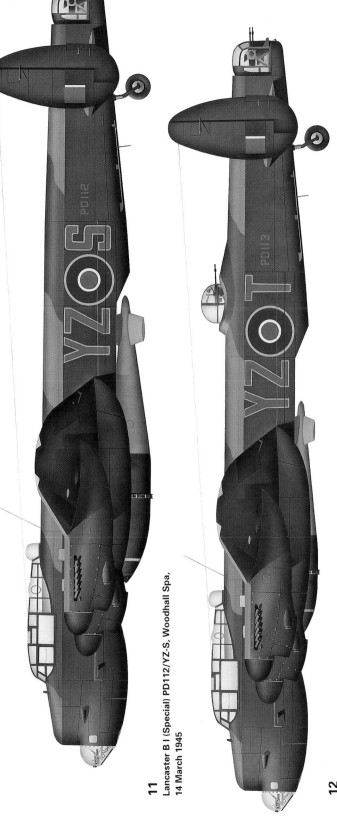

11
Lancaster B I (Special) PD112/YZ-S, Woodhall Spa,
14 March 1945

12
Lancaster B I (Special) PD113/YZ-T, Woodhall Spa, 19 March 1945

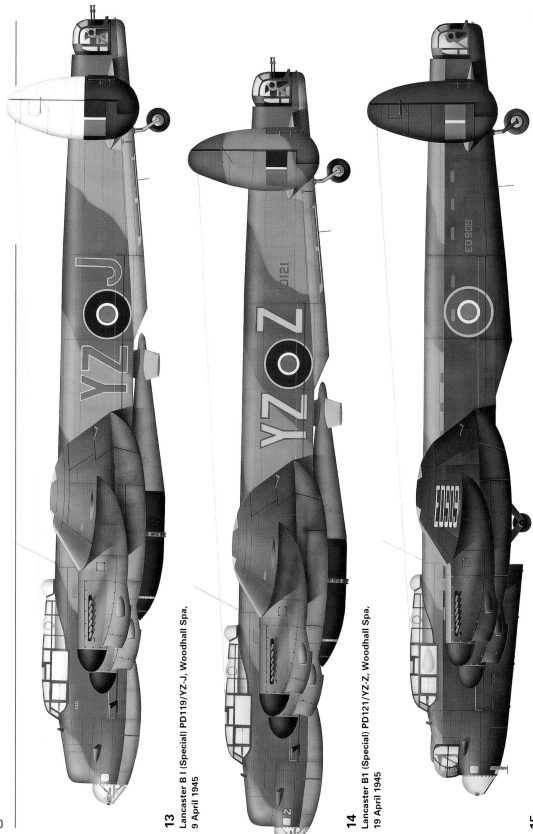

40

13

**Lancaster B I (Special) PD119/YZ-J, Woodhall Spa,
9 April 1945**

14

**Lancaster B1 (Special) PD121/YZ-Z, Woodhall Spa,
19 April 1945**

15

Lancaster B III Type 464 Provisioning ED909 of the Station Flight, Scampton, October 1946

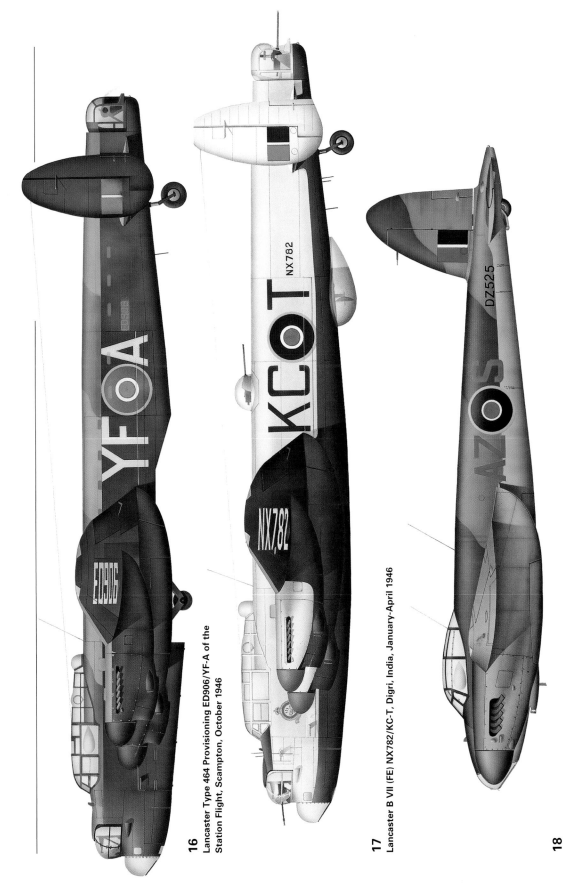

16
Lancaster Type 464 Provisioning ED906/YF-A of the
Station Flight, Scampton, October 1946

17
Lancaster B VII (FE) NX782/KC-T, Digri, India, January–April 1946

18
Mosquito FB IV DZ525/AZ-S of No 627 Sqn, Woodhall Spa, June 1944

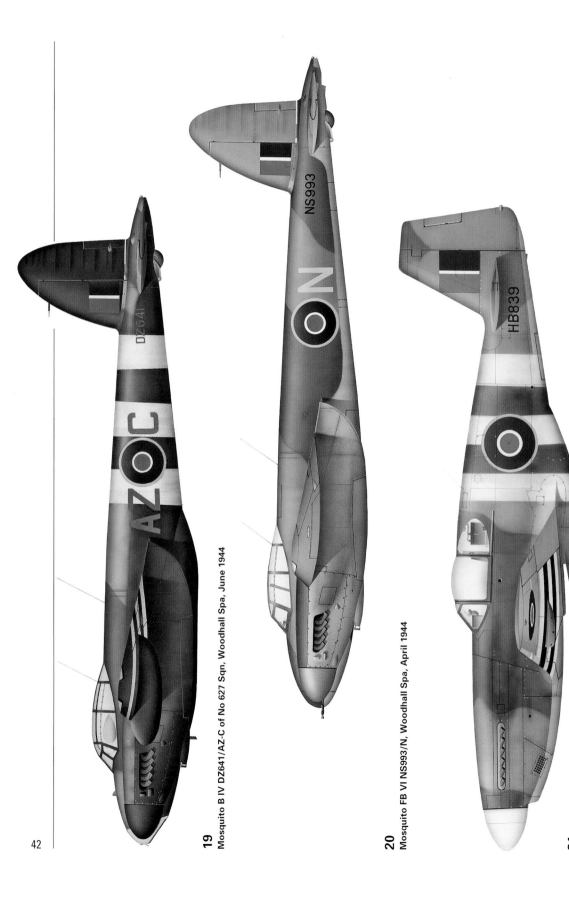

42

19
Mosquito B IV DZ641/AZ-C of No 627 Sqn, Woodhall Spa, June 1944

20
Mosquito FB VI NS993/N, Woodhall Spa, April 1944

21
Mustang III HB839, Woodhall Spa, 6 July 1944

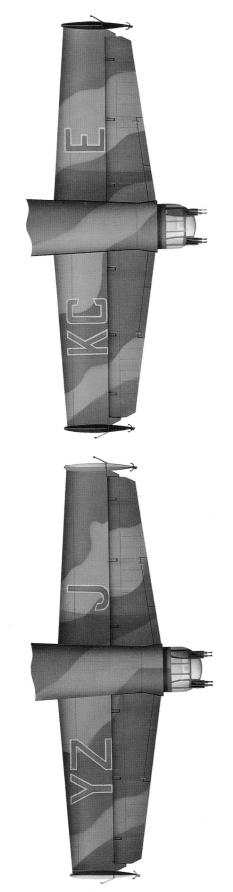

Scrap view of tailplane (upper), Lancaster B I NG445/KC-E, November 1944

Scrap view of tailplane (upper), Lancaster B I (Special) PD119/YZ-J, March 1945

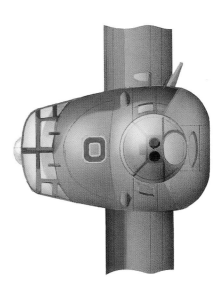

Scrap view of nose fairing, Lancaster B I (Special) PD129/YZ-O, March 1945

Scrap view of tailplane (lower), Lancaster B I (Special) PD119/YZ-J, March 1945

Approved No 617 Sqn Unit Badge

The badge design includes the words: SQUADRON · ROYAL AIR FORCE · DCXVII · DCXVII · ALTER THE MAP

Rejected No 617 Sqn Unit Badge

THE CHESHIRE ERA

As the third week of October 1943 began, No 5 Group informed Mick Martin that he was to stand down from his position as temporary commander of No 617 Sqn, as a permanent replacement had been found. A few days later, on the 25th, the highly decorated Wg Cdr Leonard Cheshire arrived, although he did not officially assume command for several weeks.

Cheshire was well known within Bomber Command, and acknowledged as a fine pilot and leader. He had gained his wings in December 1939, having learnt to fly in the Oxford University Air Squadron. Cheshire's first operational tour commenced in June 1940 with No 102 Sqn, which was equipped with Whitleys. During one operation in November 1940, his aircraft had been torn open down the length of the fuselage by a flare that had ignited inside the bomber, but he had pressed on and attacked the target nevertheless. Cheshire was awarded a DSO for his actions.

Embarking on a second tour immediately after his first (with Halifax-equipped No 35 Sqn), Cheshire had received a DFC and a second DSO for 'outstanding leadership and skill on operations' by the time he left the unit. After a short spell as an instructor, Cheshire began a third tour with No 76 Sqn in August 1942, before being promoted to group captain and elevated to Station Commander of RAF Marston Moor in March 1943. He joined No 617 Sqn seven months later.

Before October was out another flying accident occurred when, on the 30th, Plt Off Nicky Ross hit some trees in poor visibility during a low flying exercise. No one on board was hurt but two engines were badly damaged. After returning to Coningsby, the aircraft (Mick Martin's 'Dambuster' ED909/AJ-P) was officially classified Category AC, with the cause put down to Ross' 'inexperience and keenness'.

As No 617 Sqn was now fully equipped with standard Lancasters, the question of what to do with the 14 'Dambuster' type aircraft was debated. Although the highly modified bombers were only being used for occasional training flights, the execution of another 'Dambuster' operation had yet to be fully discounted, so these machines were expected to be available at short notice. This, however, left No 617 Sqn with almost double the intended allocation of Lancasters, which in turn created a great deal of work for the groundcrews.

Enquiries were made about re-converting some of the modified aircraft back to standard configuration, but ACM Harris, in a letter dated 10 October 1943, deemed that for the foreseeable future they should remain in their present state in readiness for any proposed operation. However, four days later he did agree that six could be fitted with the Stabilised Automatic Bomb Sight (SABS), which could be used in training. The SABS contained a gyroscope, and was a big improvement over other sights then in use.

In early November 1943, Harris again addressed the question of re-converting the remaining modified Lancasters. Although several new

A youthful looking Wg Cdr (Geoffrey) Leonard Cheshire, who took over command of No 617 Sqn in October 1943. Cheshire was already one of the best and most well known pilots within Bomber Command, and he went on to pioneer new marking and bombing techniques with No 617 Sqn. By the time this photograph was taken in August 1944, he was a veteran of 100 operations, and the holder of three DSOs and a DFC. Cheshire was subsequently awarded a VC too (*Sir Leonard Cheshire*)

targets had been proposed for attack with *Upkeep* (in particular the Bissorte Dam just inside the French/Italian border, and a series of four small dams between Trento and Fortezza, in Italy) nothing had been finalised. A report dated 13 November 1943 recommended, therefore, that unless a firm decision to attack the Bissorte Dam was quickly made, the aircraft should be converted back to standard form to allow No 617 Sqn to use them on normal operations.

By the end of the month the planned attack on the Bissorte Dam had been dropped, and so permission for some of them to be re-converted was approved. By 7 December it was reported that six of the 'Dambusters' had been partially re-converted 'within the unit' to carry the 12,000-lb HC bomb. The re-conversion largely involved the installation of a mid-upper turret and the removal of the special hydraulic motor, bomb-bay fairings and calliper arms, which were replaced with bulged bomb-bay doors. Sgt Bill Hume, mid-upper gunner to 'Bunny' Clayton, later recalled 'they brought the "Lanc" back to normal except for the bomb-bay doors, which they had to make deeper'. After the work was completed the six were given KC codes and allocated to specific crews as per normal.

On 11 November, the day after Cheshire properly assumed command of No 617 Sqn, the unit was scheduled for another operation to the Antheor Viaduct. This time ten aircraft took part, led by Martin, with each carrying a single 12,000-lb HC bomb. The force included five of the reconverted 'Dambusters'.

As with the previous attempt on this target, little opposition was encountered over the viaduct. Nevertheless, most of the bombs either overshot or undershot, despite the unit using the SABS. Brown bombed a railway bridge and the embankments further down the line with some success, after which all the aircraft flew on to Blida again. They left on 15 November for Coningsby, stopping off at Rabat, in Morocco, for three days on the way back. The final leg of the flight saw crews flying

Lancaster ED912/AJ-N, flown by Les Knight on the Dams raid, is seen here with Flt Lt Terry Kearns and his crew in early October 1943. A few weeks later it was returned to near standard configuration, with the removal of most of the Dambuster equipment, and the addition of a mid-upper turret and bomb-bay doors. At the same time it was given a new code of KC-S to add to the 'Saint' nose-art — a common feature on all aircraft flown by Kearns (*Tom Clarkson*)

Flt Lt Ken Brown's crew are seen at Woodhall Spa in January 1944 with their regular Lancaster DV394/KC-M. From the top, left, is Sgt Harry Hewstone (wireless operator), Plt Off Dudley Heal (navigator), Flt Sgt Don Buntaine (mid-upper gunner) and Flt Sgt Feneron (flight engineer, at top of ladder). Standing, from left to right, are WO Steve Oancia (bomb aimer), Flt Lt Ken Brown (pilot) and WO Grant McDonald (rear gunner) (*Gordon Hewstone*)

around the coast of neutral Portugal and across the Bay of Biscay, and several reported seeing an aircraft ditch in the sea, although no one had radioed that they were in trouble. The missing Lancaster was flown by Flt Lt Ted Youseman, who had joined No 617 Sqn on 26 July. No trace of the crew was ever found.

The next few weeks proved to be a frustrating time for No 617 Sqn. On no fewer than five occasions (25 November and 1-4 December) operations were scheduled then cancelled, all falling victim to poor weather. Even training was affected by the incessant rain and low cloud.

It was during this period of inactivity that Cheshire was asked to supply three crews to RAF Tempsford, near Cambridge, for special duties, which was almost certainly because of their low-flying experience. On 9 December, Clayton, Bull and a new crew (led by Canadian Flg Off Gordon Weeden, posted in at the end of September) flew down to Tempsford with 16 groundcrew, this flight having been postponed from the previous day again because of the weather. Once there, they were briefed to drop containers of arms and ammunition to the resistance near the French town of Doullens the following night.

The two 'Special Duties' units based at Tempsford (Nos 138 and 161 Sqns, both equipped with Halifax Vs) were normally tasked with missions such as this one, but they were already fully committed to other similar operations. Accompanying the crews to Tempsford was Flt Lt McCarthy in his then usual DV246/KC-U *UNCLE CHUCK CHUCK*, although he was not scheduled to fly to France. Instead, he landed at RAF Henlow the next day in a flight that he described in his logbook as 'bombing at Henlow', returning to Coningsby on the 11th. Based at Henlow was No 13 Maintenance Unit (MU), which carried out minor modifications to the bomber, as well as effecting repairs.

While this was being done, Clayton, Weeden and Bull prepared for the operation to France. They left Tempsford in the early evening on 10 December and crossed the sea, before turning south. As they neared

Flg Off Gordon Weeden and crew, who were lost on their first operation with No 617 Sqn — an attempted arms drop to French resistance fighters near Doullens — on 10 December 1943. They were flying ED825, which Flt Lt Joe McCarthy had used as AJ-T in his attack on the Sorpe Dam. It was subsequently converted to near standard configuration and recoded KC-E. In the back row, from left to right, are WO Cummings (rear gunner), Sgt Robinson (front gunner), Flg Offs Weeden (pilot) and Jones (navigator) and Flt Sgt Walters (bomb aimer). Sat in the front row are Sgt Richardson (flight engineer) and Flt Sgt Howell (wireless operator) (*Gordon Weeden*)

Doullens (15 miles north of Amiens) at very low-level, Weeden (in ED825/KC-E) was engaged by a mobile flak gun based near the town's railway station. The aircraft was hit and immediately caught fire, so Weeden banked to starboard, struggling to gain height. This manoeuvre was performed in vain, however, for ED825 struck a hill that rose on the edge of town. The six men in the forward section of the bomber were killed almost instantly, while the rear gunner, WO Robert Cummings (an American in the Royal Canadian Air Force), was found very badly injured several hundred yards from the crash. He died the following day.

Trailing Weeden's aircraft by a few minutes was 'Chuffy' Bull in ED886/KC-O. He had taken off from Tempsford almost 40 minutes after Weeden, but had made up a lot of time over the sea. Approaching Doullens, he and his crew met a similar fate, being hit by the same flak battery as they passed over the town. Although one of the petrol tanks was hit and set on fire, luck was on Bull's side as he managed to get the aircraft up to around 800 ft, avoiding the hill that had claimed his colleague. Five of the crew, including Bull, escaped by parachute at very low-level before the aircraft crashed a few miles further on. However, the wireless operator, who had been in the mid-upper turret at the time, helping to search for the drop-zone, and the rear gunner both died.

Clayton, meanwhile, who had taken off first in ED906/KC-J, had a less eventful trip. Although the No 617 Sqn Operations Book notes that the crew was unable to locate the drop zone, Clayton and his men recorded it in their logbooks as a 'good trip', returning to Tempsford without further incident. The following morning Clayton and crew returned to Coningsby, but within hours they were ordered back to Tempsford. Over the next few days they flew backwards and forwards between Coningsby and Tempsord twice, on each occasion staying overnight at the latter, flying night exercises so that they could practice finding drop zones lit only by hand-held torches on the ground.

On 20 December Clayton made another attempt to drop supplies over Doullens, accompanied by Ken Brown, Joe McCarthy and Flg Off Nicky Ross, who were officially attached to No 138 Sqn for several days. But they fared no better than the first time. Leaving Tempsford at 0115 hrs with a similar load as before, all four crews returned with their precious cargoes intake, having failed to locate the target. Dejected, they flew back to Coningsby the following day.

While the supply drops were taking place, the rest of No 617 Sqn carried out two operations. The first of these was against V1 sites at Flixecourt, in France, on 16 December. The V1 was a small pilotless 'flying bomb' that carried an explosive payload. When its fuel supply was exhausted the bomb fell to earth and exploded. The V1 was the first of several 'vengeance' weapons that the Germans had begun planning and constructing in June 1942.

This was the first mainstream operation for No 617 Sqn in almost five weeks, and the first that Cheshire would lead. Accompanying the unit was a single *Oboe*-equipped Mosquito that was to mark the target for No 617 Sqn to bomb on. Nine aircraft, including two reconverted Dams Lancasters, took off from 1700 hrs, and although their bombing was accurate (an average error of only 94 yards, with two crews managing an incredible 30 yards), the initial marking was poor, being dropped almost 350 yards from the centre of the aiming point. As a result, the target remained largely undamaged.

Four nights later, on the 20th, eight crews (including two new replacements) flew to Leige, in Belgium, to attack an armaments factory. This operation was again to be preceded by Pathfinders, but as with the mission on the 16th, the marking failed – very few of the target markers were visible to the crews preparing to bomb. With heavy flak and reported fighter activity, Cheshire decided after 25 minutes over the target that it was useless and aborted the operation.

After turning for home, Geoff Rice (in EE150/KC-Z) was attacked by a fighter, which continued to fire as they began falling from 14,000 ft. Watching crews reported seeing the rear gunner, Sgt Stephen 'Ginger' Burns, valiantly return fire all the while, but to no avail. Only Rice managed to escape by parachute as the aircraft broke up, waking up in a wood a few hours later with a broken wrist and his parachute spread amongst the trees. After a few months on the run, he was eventually captured and taken prisoner.

The remaining six members of Rice's crew perished, although a later Belgian Police report indicated that the wireless operator, WO Bruce Gowrie, had survived, only to be shot by German soldiers whilst trying to escape. However, this contradicts Canadian reports, which suggest that he died as the aircraft crashed.

The rest of the squadron landed back at Coningsby with their bomb loads intact, except for Dick Willsher (one of the new crews), who had jettisoned his over the target.

As 1943 drew to a close, No 617 Sqn was sent on operations twice more. On the 22nd, 11 crews attacked the V1 site near Abbeville, in the Pas de Calais area of France, and on the 30th ten crews returned to the V1 site at Flixecourt. Both times the marking was either poor or the flares burned for so short a time that the crews were not able to bomb on them. During the Abbeville mission, Cheshire circled the target for 15 minutes after the attack was due to have ended before finally ordering the squadron back to base without bombing. Crews did get their ordnance away during the second raid, with slightly better results than those achieved on the 16th, but again it was unsatisfactory.

NEW YEAR AND NEW TECHNIQUES

As the New Year dawned, Cheshire reflected on the squadron's achievements. It had carried out 16 operations since being formed nine months earlier, which had resulted in the loss of 14 crews, including the squadron commander and four flight commanders. More recent missions had been so poor that on more than one occasion the unit had returned without bombing at all.

Cheshire began to think of ways in which the target marking could be improved, and suggested to AVM Cochrane at No 5 Group that perhaps it could be done at very low-level instead. Cochrane disagreed, considering it too hazardous, and instead suggested that it might be better from about 5000 ft, which, if accurate, should provide enough of a mark for the rest of the squadron to bomb on. Cheshire reluctantly conceded, but in turn asked that No 617 Sqn be allowed to mark its own targets and dispense with the Pathfinders, to which Cochrane agreed.

The first operation of the year for No 617 Sqn came on 4 January, when 11 crews flew to the Pas de Calais again to attack the V1 sites. Most aircraft were carrying a load of 14 1000-lb bombs, although the two re-converted 'Dambusters' in the force carried only 11 apiece due to the previous structural alterations. Arriving over the target area, crews were met by heavy cloud and thick smoke from the marker flares, which drifted and did not properly light the target.

Sqn Ldr Bill Suggitt (who had been posted in from No 428 Sqn at the end of October 1943 to take command of A Flight) was unable to bomb because of a faulty bombsight, while some of the others had to make more than one run over the target before they could see enough to aim at. Plt Off Nicky Ross gave up after two runs and turned for home with his load still aboard.

Cheshire had a passenger with him that evening in the form of Grp Capt 'Tiny' Evans-Evans (universally known as 'Evans Squared'), the Station Commander at RAF Coningsby. It was his last chance to fly with No 617 Sqn, as the unit had received word that it was to move base again. On 7 January an advanced party travelled to RAF Woodhall Spa, a few miles away from Coningsby, with the rest of the unit following on two days later.

Crews had little time to settle in to their new home before operations were scheduled for them again on the 10th. However, poor weather saw a cancellation, which was repeated on the 14th for the same reason. Nevertheless, squadron personnel were kept busy with lectures, an escape and evasion exercise (on the 16th) and the usual round of training flights. During a take-off in 'Dambuster' ED933/AJ-X for one such mission on the 13th, Cheshire hit a flock of plovers, leading him to note in his logbook 'collected 20 bodies for consumption in the mess'!

On 20 January operations were detailed, and cancelled, yet again. So instead, six crews took off at dusk in modified Lancasters for some

Flt Lt Tom O'Shaughnessy (left) with his crew in the summer of 1943. The remaining personnel are, from left to right, Flg Off Kendrick (bomb aimer), Flt Sgt Ward (wireless operator), WO Hutton (rear gunner), Sgt Stewart (flight engineer), Sgt Holt (mid-upper gunner) and (kneeling) Flg Off Holding (navigator). During the evening of 20 January 1944, whilst engaged on a practice flight in Dambuster ED918/AJ-F, O'Shaughnessy crashed. He and Holding were killed instantly, while Kendrick and Ward suffered serious injuries. The remaining three aircrew missed the fatal flight (*Ray Fisher*)

low-level 'Dambuster' bombing practice over The Wash, although due to a mix-up Flt Lt Tom O'Shaughnessy left in ED918/AJ-F with only three of his crew aboard. The group duly set course for Snettisham, on the southern edge of The Wash near Kings Lynn, and prepared to begin the exercise.

As O'Shaughnessy commenced his initial run in, tragedy struck. Descending lower than the prescribed 60 ft, the Lancaster glanced the sea and, out of control, crashed onto the beach before hitting the sea wall and bursting into flames. O'Shaughnessy and his navigator, Flg Off Arthur Holding, were killed instantly and bomb aimer Flg Off George Kendrick (who had been in the nose of the bomber at the time) was severely injured. The wireless operator, Plt Off Arthur Ward, was thrown out of the aircraft as it came to rest, sustaining severe bruising, a dislocated right elbow and a broken left arm.

Putting this tragedy behind them, crews were were briefed for another operation to the V1 sites in the Pas de Calais the following night. For the first time, Cheshire illuminated the target in a Lancaster (DV380/KC-N), releasing his spot fires (markers) from 7000 ft. Although the initial bombing was good, the flares were already going out by the time the last crews commenced their runs (or made a second run), and a number of them returned with partial bomb loads. The unit tried again on the 25th but results were inconclusive, despite Cheshire marking this time from just over 5300 ft.

The damaged inflicted during these mission convinced Cheshire that very low-level marking was the answer to accurate pinpoint bombing, especially if low cloud obscured the target. However, during a practice exercise over The Wash, Mick Martin had tried dive-bombing his Lancaster, aiming visually and without using the bombsight, and he had achieved very accurate results. Cheshire tried it himself on 29 January with equally good results and, convinced it could work, went to see Cochrane.

Although the No 5 Group commander could see a number of benefits to the method, he was still reluctant to allow the crews to use it because of the extreme risk they would be exposed to. Cheshire countered his objections by arguing that it would actually reduce the risk, as the aircraft concerned would only spend a very short time at that height, having dived from a higher level. There were other advantages too. Any markers dropped after diving were unlikely to skid off the target as they might do if expended by aircraft flying in already at that height.

His persistence paid off and Cochrane gave his authorisation for No 617 Sqn to try the new marking method on their next operation, which was to be to the Gnome-Rhône aero engine factories at Limoges, in France, the following night. The target presented another problem though. It was staffed by French civilian labour, and the political implications would be extremely serious if No 617 Sqn was seen to be wantonly bombing innocent civilians.

Aside from the marking, Cheshire had also been giving some thought to the possible filming of operations for later analysis. He had become aware of a Sqn Ldr Pat Moyna of the RAF Film Unit (RAFFU), and invited him over to Woodhall Spa at the end of January to discuss some ideas. Moyna had been with the RAFFU for more than two years, working primarily on training and public relations films. He too had seen the potential benefit of making operational films during raids, spending many months trying to gain support, but generally without success. Moyna was therefore delighted to receive Cheshire's invitation.

The two men walked around the airfield talking for an hour or so before Cheshire asked Moyna if he thought he could film a 'live' operation. Moyna replied that given the right facilities, he was sure it could be done. Arrangements were quickly made for two cameras to be

Sqn Ldr Pat Moyna examines a spool of film with WAAF Sgt Barrie Monteney at No 1 RAF Film Unit, at RAF Stanmore Park, in November 1944. After discussing with Wg Cdr Cheshire the possibility of filming live operations for later analysis, Moyna was invited to fly with No 617 Sqn on operations from February of that year (*IWM Neg No CH14175*)

fitted to Cheshire's Lancaster, with one pointing down through the rear fuselage to capture a picture behind the aircraft (using mirrors in what was known as a 'vertical mirror camera') and the other mounted on the inside of the rear entry door, filming obliquely through a hole cut in the door's wooden skin. Moyna thought that the Lancaster looked more like a small studio than a bomber once fully rigged up.

On 8 February 1944, 12 aircraft left Woodhall Spa and set course for Limoges, with Moyna on board Cheshire's Lancaster (DV380/KC-N) with his cameras. The target was hidden in a valley and hard to spot, but as they arrived, Cheshire flew in low over the factory three times to warn the civilian workers of the impending attack (thus giving them time to make for the shelters), before diving again to release his incendiary markers, which he recorded later as 'dead centre at 50 ft'.

Being so low he almost caused his own demise, for the markers hit the roof and bounced up, nearly striking the tail of his aircraft, before they ignited and fell away again. Immediately, all the lights within the complex, and the nearby town, went out. Martin (the deputy leader) flew in a few minutes later to drop incendiaries to enhance the flares, with the rest of the squadron ordered in to bomb immediately after the latter had cleared the target.

Cheshire kept a series of personal journals detailing the operations he flew with No 617 Sqn, and in them he noted that the last crew to bomb (Plt Off Ross) on this mission dropped their ordnance 'apparently in the same crater as Flt Lt Shannon', who had bombed first. After ordering the rest of the crews home, he and Martin flew down low over the target, inspecting the results and machine-gunning the sheds. Moyna filmed the scene from the door-mounted camera, before they too headed back to the UK.

Once back at Woodhall, Moyna's film was eagerly examined. The marking had been pinpoint and the overall results exceptional, with 21

A cine camera of the type first used by Sqn Ldr Pat Moyna during the attack on the Gnome-Rhône aero engine factories on 8 February 1944. A second camera filmed a downward rear view during the marking run. This Lancaster (PD337/JO-V) was later used by the No 5 Group Film Unit, and it filmed many of No 617 Sqn's operations in late 1944 and early 1945, including the attacks on the *Tirpitz*

This remarkable photograph was taken by Pat Moyna using the 'vertical mirror' cine-camera mounted in Wg Cdr Cheshire's Lancaster DV380/KC-N during the raid on the Gnome-Rhône aero engine factories on 8 February 1944. The incendiary markers dropped by Cheshire hit the roof of the factory, before bouncing up and igniting, silhouetting the tail-wheel of his aircraft in the top centre of the image (*IWM Neg No HU93014*)

of the 48 bays within the factory complex having been completely destroyed and the rest severely damaged. Cheshire's idea of low-level marking was proved to the extent that Sir Charles Portal (Chief of the Air Staff) was moved to comment to ACM Harris, 'I have just seen the photographs of the Gnome- Rhône aero engine factory at Limoges taken after an attack on 8-9 February by No 617 Sqn. The very severe damage caused by so small a number of aircraft is most remarkable, and I should be grateful if you would convey my warmest congratulations to this squadron on the extreme accuracy of their bombing'.

Bad weather prevented operations over the next few days, but on 12 February the unit was detailed for another attempt on the Antheor

A vertical reconnaissance photograph of the Gnome-Rhône aero engine plant the morning after the attack on 8 February 1944. The incredible accuracy obtained through the low-level marking is clearly evident by the destruction of some sheds, while the workers' canteen remains almost untouched. Wg Cdr Cheshire flew across the site from top right to bottom left, dropping his incendiary markers (seen in the photograph above) on the sheds in the top row (*IWM Neg No HU92970*)

Sqn Ldr Mick Martin and crew, with their Lancaster DV402/KC-P *Popsie*, at Woodhall Spa in late January 1944. During the 12 February 1944 raid on the Antheor Viaduct, the aircraft was hit by flak, which injured flight engineer Ivan Whittaker and killed bomb aimer Bob Hay. These men are, from left to right, Flt Lt 'Tammy' Simpson (rear gunner), Flg Off Ken Stott (navigator), Flg Off Toby Foxlee (mid-upper gunner), Sqn Ldr Mick Martin (pilot), Flt Lt Ivan Whittaker (flight engineer) and Flt Lt Bob Hay (bomb aimer) (*Georgina Whittaker*)

American personnel discussing the damage to Martin's DV402/KC-P after it had landed in Sardinia following the attack on the Antheor Viaduct on 12 February 1944. The flak strike that killed bomb aimer Bob Hay and injured flight engineer Ivan Whittaker left a hole in the nose, which can be clearly seen below the turret. Martin was flying almost level with the gun at the time (*Georgina Whittaker*)

Viaduct. Eleven crews, all carrying a single 12,000-lb HC bomb, would take part, while Cheshire carried spot fires and incendiaries for target identification. Because the Lancasters would be operating at the limit of their range, and the poor weather was expected to leave only two bases in the UK available for landing when they returned, Cheshire asked for permission to fly on to Sardinia instead. However, to his dismay, this was denied, leaving him to note in his journal 'this permission was refused, categorically and without qualification'. Instead, the crews were detailed to land at RAF Ford, on the south coast, where they would refuel before setting out.

Flying down with the unit as far as Ford was Grp Capt Johnson, Commanding Officer of Woodhall Spa, and Sqn Ldr 'Tommy' Lloyd, the Station Intelligence Officer, who would debrief them upon their return.

As No 617 Sqn approached the viaduct, the unit found it defended by searchlights and a dozen heavy and numerous light flak guns. The whole area was also blanketed by low cloud, which made positive identification difficult from above 3000 ft. Cheshire and Martin both made several runs but were engaged by the defences each time, Cheshire eventually dropping his markers on a nearby beach. Although he instructed the rest of the crews to alter their bombing accordingly, most over- or undershot. But worse was to come.

Mick Martin flew in very low to get his back-up markers nearer the aiming point, clearing the viaduct by only 50 ft as he passed over it. But as he did so his aircraft was holed by a shell from a 20 mm flak gun based near the target, hitting bomb aimer Flt Lt Bob Hay and flight engineer Flt Lt

The Antheor Viaduct, seen here pre-war, was surrounded by steep hills. This photograph clearly gives an indication of the difficulty facing the crews who marked it at low-level. After dropping his markers during the operation on 12 February 1944, Sqn Ldr Mick Martin cleared the viaduct by only 50 ft, his Lancaster being hit by flak in the process

Ivan Whittaker. Martin struggled to control the aircraft and aborted the operation, flying out over the sea and out of range, before turning for Sardinia. On the way he experienced icing, a stalled engine and a bomb 'hang up', but he eventually landed his crippled Lancaster at an American base, where Whittaker was admitted to the station hospital with leg wounds. For Bob Hay, however, it was too late, the initial flak burst having killed him instantly. Hay had been the unit's bombing leader for the Dams raid, and was an immensely popular member of No 617 Sqn.

The operation had been a total failure, which Cheshire put down to inaccurate information about the defences, and insufficient petrol reserves that prevented him from being able to fly freely around the target to control the attack. He also noted scathingly in his journal 'no photos taken, as the armoury loaded all aircraft with recce flares instead of photoflashes by mistake'.

The rest of the squadron returned to Ford in the early hours, where they were debriefed by Lloyd before breaking for breakfast. As dawn broke to heavy rain and patchy fog, most of the crews decided to remain where they were until it cleared. Bill Suggitt thought that he could reach Woodhall, however, and he offered Lloyd a lift, which he accepted after first having a wash and shave. By the time they eventually took off, the weather had worsened further, and ten minutes later, in driving rain, Suggitt clipped a tree and crashed into a hill. His aircraft (DV382/KC-J) disintegrated upon impact, killing seven of those on board, including Lloyd and flight engineer Flt Sgt John Pulford (who had flown with Gibson on the Dams raid). Bill Suggitt, seriously injured, was taken to hospital in Chichester, where he died on 15 February without regaining consciousness.

On 23 February Martin arrived back at Woodhall Spa from Blida, in North Africa, where his aircraft had been repaired. The crew had flown there from Sardinia with the undercarriage down because of the bomber's damaged hydraulics, but not before Bob Hay had been buried in the local cemetery in Cagliari.

BACK TO FACTORY-BUSTING

On 1 March No 617 Sqn was detailed for an operation to Albert, in northern France, where it would attack the BMW engine factory and GSP works. Postponed a night, the raid eventually took place on the 2nd. This was the unit's biggest operation since the Dams raid, involving 15 crews. The defences were expected to be heavy, so Cochrane insisted it be marked at medium level (around 5000 ft).

As the squadron arrived over the target, Cheshire began his run in, but his bomb-sight failed. Despite his bomb aimer attempting running repairs, the device refused to spring back into life. Waiting until the last main force target flare had begun to fade, Cheshire ordered Les Munro in to drop his markers, which he did well within the target area. Bombing by No 617 Sqn was highly accurate as a result of Munro's excellent work, the unit inflicting such severe damage that the Germans simply abandoned large parts of the factory. Subsequent output was only a tenth of what it had been before the attack, but better still, No 617 Sqn suffered no losses during the operation.

Two days later, the unit attacked the La Ricamerie needle bearing factory at St Etienne, in France. This was a small target – in fact the smallest it had yet been assigned, with the main shed only 40 yards wide by 70 yards long. Although he lost an engine soon after take-off, Munro continued to the target with the rest of the squadron, only to find ten-tenths cloud that precluded any attempt to bomb. Cheshire aborted the operation, which was particularly frustrating as the weather report had told them to expect perfect conditions.

Operations were cancelled twice more over the next few days (on the 5th and 6th) before the unit tried St Etienne again on 10 March. Again crews found it blanketed by ten-tenths cloud despite reports predicting perfect conditions, obscuring the factory from view. Cheshire was only able to catch a glimpse of the target when directly above it, so he tried several runs, diving from 500 ft down to 200 ft before releasing his incendiaries on the fifth attempt – these were considered to be more effective than standard markers under dense cloud. However, they overshot, so Cheshire instructed Munro to have a try, although his also failed, undershooting by almost a quarter-of-a-mile. Shannon attempted from a different direction, making the necessary alterations to his drop, and succeeded in placing his flares on the factory roof. The remaining crews were ordered to bomb just to one side, with the result that more than 80 per cent of the factory was destroyed.

On 15 March the target was another aero engine factory, this time at Woippy, in France. As the crews approached their run in point, they again found the target area blanketed in ten-tenths cloud, ruling out an attack. Cheshire was enraged, as he had been assured that the weather would again be clear and the target easily visible. He remarked in his journal, 'The leader restrained himself from sending a rude message back to base and ordered the squadron to return home'.

Most of the crews had an uneventful return back to the UK, but not Flg Off Warren Duffy in ME560/KC-H. His rear gunner, Flt Sgt Tom McLean, noticed that they were being shadowed by another machine.

He quickly realised that it was in fact a pair in aircraft formation, while a third was flying off their port side as a decoy. Later reports on the subsequent action are conflicting.

Post-war, McLean himself wrote that the two following aircraft were Bf 110s, both of which he succeeded in shooting down as they closed in, before realising that a third was now behind them, also preparing to attack. This too was destroyed before the mid-upper gunner, WO 'Red' Evans, fired at the decoy, which disappeared into the night, later confirmed as downed. Contemporary squadron records, however, note that the crew was 'attacked by enemy fighters. Two were claimed shot down by the mid-upper gunner', while in his personal journal Cheshire recorded that McLean 'shot down two Ju 88s and a possible Fw 190', despite being wounded in the hand.

Whatever the truth, it was an incredible feat, with two, and possibly three, enemy aircraft confirmed destroyed and another probable. By the end of 1944 McLean had added a DFC to the DFM he had won with his previous squadron, largely for his exploits on 15-16 March.

The campaign against the French factories continued the following night when 15 aircraft flew to Clermont Ferrand to attack two sites (the Michelin & Cie Tyre Factory and the Soc Gen des Etabs Bergougnan) in conjunction with six aircraft from No 106 Sqn. Lancasters from the latter unit were carrying additional navigation equipment that would help the formation locate the target. They would also be responsible for dropping the markers.

The tyre factory consisted of three large workshops and a workers' canteen, and was heavily camouflaged with netting, complete with dummy roads and installations that had been painted onto it. As before, great emphasis was placed on accurate bombing so as to eliminate the possibility of civilian casualties. Again, Cheshire began by

Flt Lt Joe McCarthy (second from left) poses with his rear gunner Flt Lt Dave Rodger (left) and navigator Flg Off Don MacLean (third from left) on the rear terrace of the Officers' Mess at the Petwood Hotel in March 1944. With them is Flt Lt Danny Walker, navigator to Flt Lt Dave Shannon. All four flew on the original Dams raid, and eventually served with No 617 Sqn for over a year (*Dave Rodger*)

flying in low to warn the workers, before releasing his spot fires, which fell short. McCarthy, Munro and Shannon followed up, dropping their markers on the roofs of the workshops, which were then bombed so accurately by the rest of the squadron that Cheshire radioed back the message 'Michelin's complexion seems a trifle red'.

As the crews returned to the UK they faced thickening fog, so many were diverted to RAF Fiskerton, where fog dispersal equipment was in operation. A measure of just how bad conditions were will be realised by the fact that the crews were taken to sleep in the Mess on base, as their quarters two miles away could not be found in the murk!

Post-raid photographs showed astounding results, with the three workshops having been totally destroyed but the workers' canteen surviving untouched. The images were so impressive that they were sent directly to the war cabinet.

With the campaign against French industry in full swing, another attack, against the powder works at Bergerac, was scheduled for 18 March. Marking was again very successful, although Munro, dropping his spot fires from 6000 ft, quickly realised that they had been fitted with fuses set to detonate at 3000 ft instead of ground level. Incendiaries dropped by the accompanying No 106 Sqn crews were scattered, but overall bombing was accurate.

On this night another new tactic was employed. 'Bunny' Clayton, in ME560/KC-H, dropped his 12,000-lb HC bomb in conjunction with a single 1000-lb bomb that was set to detonate first, exploding the larger weapon whilst just above the target. The resulting shock waves devastated a nearby munitions dump, which was completely destroyed in an explosion that Cheshire estimated 'lasted at least 15 seconds'.

A similar operation to the Poudrerie Nationale Explosives Factory at Angouleme two nights later (20 March) brought similar results, with several crews using the new technique. As No 617 Sqn left the area and headed home, Cheshire sent the simple message 'In accordance with tradition'.

The final week of March proved to be a frustrating one, with several unsuccessful attempts being made by the unit to knock out the aero engine factory at Lyons, in France. The first, on 23 March, was hampered by poor weather, while the second two days later fared little better. A third attempt on the 28th was aborted before the aircraft even left the ground because of bad weather, while another the following night was described by Cheshire as 'worse than ever' due to the flares failing to ignite. As a result the circling No 106 Sqn crews were at a loss as to what to do until Flt Lt Kearns, flying as deputy leader, ordered No 617 Sqn to drop any remaining flares they had. From then on the bombing was well concentrated, allowing Cheshire to radio back the signal 'All bombs within white square' – a light-hearted reference to an order from Harris that all bombs had to fall within a white square marked on the target map at briefing.

At the end of the month some reorganisation took place within No 617 Sqn that saw the unit's crews split into three flights from the previous two. Shannon and McCarthy were both promoted to squadron leader, joining Munro in commanding them.

MOSQUITOS

Although Leonard Cheshire's low-level marking theory had now been proved using Lancasters, he had felt for some time that the mission was better suited to a smaller, more agile aircraft. No 617 Sqn had already flown operations with Mosquitos as fighter escorts, and it was this aircraft that Cheshire was interested in. Known as the 'Wooden Wonder' because it was made entirely of plywood, the Mosquito was both fast and manoeuvrable, making it ideally suited to the job.

On 19 December 1943, Cheshire had visited Grp Capt Percy Pickard, CO of No 161 Sqn and a known low-flying expert. They discussed the merits of the Mosquito at length before Pickard took Cheshire up for a 20-minute flight in one to demonstrate how it handled. The latter was impressed, and the following week he went to the Air Ministry to see Air Commodore 'Charles' Whitworth, who was on the staff of the Operations Directorate. Whitworth had been the Station Commander at RAF Scampton when No 617 Sqn was formed, and was an old family friend of Cheshire's. He had also been Cheshire's first flying instructor when he joined the Oxford University Air Squadron.

Cheshire asked Whitworth how easy it might be to get hold of a couple of Mosquitos if he needed them, to which he received the reply that first he must convince Cochrane of their usefulness before going any further. As already detailed in the previous chapter of this book, Cochrane had initially refused the idea of low-level marking so the plan had been dropped. However, now that it had been proved using Lancasters, Cheshire tried again, asking if he might have one or two

Grp Capt 'Charles' Whitworth was the Station Commander at Scampton when No 617 Sqn was formed. A pre-war friend of Leonard Cheshire, he was an air commodore working at the Air Ministry when he helped Cheshire obtain several Mosquitos for No 617 Sqn to use in a low-level marking role (*Joan Whitworth*)

61

Mosquitos on standby if he needed them. Cochrane rethought the plan, and with the agreement of ACM Harris, two were loaned to the unit from 27 March 1944 for a month.

Both aircraft (ML975/HS-M and ML976/HS-N) were Mosquito XVIs with pressurised cabins for high-altitude flying. Borrowed from No 109 Sqn, ML974 was flown by Cheshire for the first time on 30 March. The next day he took ML975 over to Swinderby and flew it locally for almost an hour, before returning to base.

Cheshire was now a happy man. From the dark days of heavy losses when he took over No 617 Sqn, the unit was now operating with minimal casualties, while bombing accuracy had improved greatly. Cheshire had developed low-level marking techniques, which could be expanded with the two Mosquitos he now had, and Moyna's films allowed for post-raid analysis. To top it all off, news came through on 2 April that he had been awarded a third DSO.

The first opportunity to see what could be done in a Mosquito came three days later when No 617 Sqn was detailed to attack an aircraft repair depot at Toulouse, in France, as part of a No 5 Group force numbering 144 aircraft. Cheshire would fly in first in ML976/HS-N to alert the French workers, before dropping his spot fires from 800 ft. Two Lancasters would follow up with further markers, before the main force proceeded to bomb.

As the Mosquito would be operating at the very limit of its range, Cheshire sought advice from the aircraft's manufacturers, and was duly visited by John de Havilland himself that morning. After some discussion, he told Cheshire that as the Mk XVI was designed for high altitude flight, he thought that the distance to the target when flown at low-level would exceed the aircraft's range on internal fuel only. Cheshire thought hard about the implications, but having argued to get the aircraft in the first place, decided to try anyway.

On his own admission, Cheshire's inexperience on the type contributed to his arriving six minutes late over the target. But he still made two runs, before releasing four markers on the third, narrowly avoiding the heavy flak as he wheeled away from the area. The main force bombing was extremely accurate, which was particularly notable, as most crews had had no training in interpreting the new marking technique. In fact, the results were so good that only hours after seeing photographs of the damage, Harris informed Cochrane that No 5 Group could act as an independent unit from then on, marking their own targets. To supplement this he transferred two Pathfinder squadrons (Nos 83 and 97) back to No 5 Group, as well as a Mosquito squadron (No 627), which would be based alongside No 617 Sqn at Woodhall Spa.

The day after the Toulouse raid, yet another weapon was added to the No 617 Sqn armoury in the form of an airborne radar system known as H2S, which was able to distinguish between land and water. Although basic by today's standards, it allowed crews to bomb blind through haze, smoke or heavy cloud. Six H2S-equipped Lancasters were flown in by crews joining No 617 Sqn.

The unit's next target was a German signals equipment depot at St Cyr, in France, which Bomber Command decided 'had to be destroyed at all costs'. When the depot was attacked on 10 April, No

Plt Off Freddy Watts in the cockpit of ND554 *Conquering Cleo* – a name derived from the code letters LE-C, which the bomber wore when assigned to No 630 Sqn. *Cleo* was one of six Lancasters equipped with H2S that were loaned to No 617 Sqn in April 1944. Flown over to the unit by Watts when he joined, it was given the new codes KC-<u>N</u>, before returning to No 630 Sqn on 10 June that same year (*Freddy Watts*)

617 Sqn despatched several newly arrived pilots, navigators and bomb aimers from the H2S crews so that they could observe the marking and bombing methods the unit employed. As Cheshire was marking in a Mosquito (ML976/HS-N), Moyna's cameras were fitted to Munro's regular mount (LM482/KC-W) to allow him to film it. Once over the target, Cheshire began his dive from 5000 ft, releasing two red spot fires at 1000 ft on the northwest edge of the factory complex, followed by the rest of the crews who bombed from various heights with great accuracy.

The following week proved to be a busy one for No 617 Sqn. While the H2S crews flew numerous training exercises, David Shannon and his navigator, Flg Off Len Sumpter (who had re-mustered as a navigator after flying as Shannon's bomb aimer on the Dams raid), and Flt Lt Terry Kearns and his navigator, Flg Off Bill Barclay, went over to No 1655 (Mosquito) Training Unit at RAF Warboys for a conversion course. As most of their respective crews were now 'tour expired', they were posted out to other units for instructional duties or a rest. Amongst the latter was Sqn Ldr Danny Walker, Shannon's Canadian navigator on both Nos 106 and 617 Sqns, who was rested in preparation for a return to his homeland, having completed three operational tours. As Shannon and Kearns returned, another Mosquito crew (Flg Offs Fawke and Bennett) was posted in to supplement them.

In mid-April No 617 Sqn said goodbye to most of its remaining original 'Dambuster' aircraft. They were now being flown so infrequently that the bombers were becoming a problem to maintain. With groundcrews stretched to maintain them in an airworthy condition alongside the standard aircraft, the decision was taken to fly most of them to RAF Metheringham, ostensibly for storage. However, over the next few months they were frequently flown by No 106 Sqn, which was based there, on fighter affiliation, cross-country and general transport and air experience flights.

Sgt Ken Flatt, Flt Sgt Doug Garton and Sgt Vic Atter, groundcrew with No 627 Sqn at Woodhall Spa, pose with their motorcycles in front of Wg Cdr Cheshire's regular Mosquito NS993/N, which was one of four eventually given to No 617 Sqn on a permanent basis. Cheshire first flew this aircraft operationally on 18 April 1944 (to Juvisy), and whilst returning from Brunswick in it four days later he shot up an airfield control tower that he noticed with all of its lights on (*Doug Garton*)

Some had remained in their 'Dambuster' configuration throughout, while others had been converted back to near standard Lancaster fit, although these were returned to their modified form before departure. ED906, for example, which had been flown to the Dams by David Maltby as AJ-J, had been converted to near standard and flown on five more operations as KC-J. After returning to 'Dambuster' configuration, it too was moved to Metheringham as AJ-G.

On 18 April No 617 Sqn targeted the railway marshalling yards at Juvisy, in France, the unit being tasked with carrying out the initial illuminating, marking and bombing. It would be the first time that the squadron had used its H2S aircraft, while the four Mosquitos flying that night now included two that were permanently allocated to No 617 Sqn – NS992/S and NS993/N.

Flg Off Warren Duffy also had a passenger with him that night in the form of Air Commodore Alfred Sharpe, commander of No 54 Base. The latter had been formed in August 1943 by administratively combining the three RAF stations of Coningsby, Woodhall Spa and Metheringham. Sharpe wanted to witness the techniques used by No 617 Sqn, as well as the results they achieved. A further 200 aircraft from No 5 Group completed the force, and a considerable amount of damage was done thanks to successful target marking.

A similar operation was repeated on the 20th when the railway marshalling yards at La Chapelle, in the suburbs of Paris, were heavily bombed. This time, the four Mosquitos were supplemented by three Pathfinder squadrons and a handful of Pathfinder Mosquitos from No 8 Group that were equipped with *Oboe* (a radar locating device) in the first group-wide use of the new marking method.

The target was so large that it was considered unsuitable for a single concentrated attack, so the 14 aircraft from No 617 Sqn were split into two waves, separated by an hour, to allow the smoke and haze from the first attack to clear.

Cheshire (in Mosquito NS993/N) had a malfunction with his compass that resulted in him struggling to find the target, but the initial marking was extremely accurate, nevertheless, as was the bombing by the following main force. This was just as well, as the Senior Air Staff Officer of No 5 Group, Air Commodore Harry Satterly, was flying with Les Munro in LM482/KC-W.

BACK TO GERMANY

Since the disastrous raid against the Dortmund-Ems Canal in September 1943, all but one of the targets assigned to No 617 Sqn had been in France (the other one was in neighbouring Belgium). This had allowed the unit to perfect its low-level target marking methods – something ACM Harris was now keen to employ against targets in Germany. So in the third week of April he put the squadron on standby for an operation, the likely target being Munich, Darmstadt or Brunswick. On the 22nd No 617 Sqn received orders that it would be flying to the latter city as part of a force of 265 aircraft sent to bomb its heavily defended marshalling yards. Two No 627 Sqn Mosquitos would fly ahead to report back on the weather over the target, which, if clear, would be illuminated by Nos 83 and 97 Sqns. If heavy cloud cover blanketed the target, the Pathfinder crews would drop markers instead.

With clear skies, the target was illuminated as planned. The initial markers were dropped accurately by four No 617 Sqn Mosquitos, but the back-up markers expended by the other squadrons landed too far south. The rest of the force was unaware of this error, however, as one of the Pathfinder crews had inadvertently switched on their transmitter, jamming all communications. The resultant bombing was widespread, with little damage done to the target itself. Cheshire consoled himself on the way home by shooting up an airfield control tower that he noticed was 'advertising itself' by having all of its lights on. Although the overall operation had been unsuccessful, No 617 Sqn's marking had been accurate, so two days later Bomber Command tried the same tactic again, but this time over the marshalling yards at Munich.

The latter city boasted a major rail junction, with much traffic from eastern France and southwest Germany running through it, as well as lines connecting Italy with northern Germany. Like Brunswick, the Munich marshalling yards were also heavily defended, so to divert attention from the main attack, six crews would carry out a 'spoof' raid over Milan, dropping flares and target indicators to simulate an imminent attack there.

Mosquito DZ641/AZ-C is serviced at Woodhall Spa in the summer of 1944. On 22 June Sqn Ldr David Shannon flew this aircraft on the aborted attack on the V1 site at Wizernes, in France, being recalled on the outward flight. DZ641 was struck off charge on 19 January 1946 (*Brian Harris*)

No 617 Sqn contributed 12 Lancasters and four Mosquitos to a main force of 260 aircraft. The Mosquitos would be operating at the very limit of their range, as supplementary drop tanks were not available. In an effort to maximise their endurance, the Mosquitos initially flew down to Manston, on the north Kent coast, in order to refuel, before setting off again some two hours after the rest of the squadron.

Once over the target area, Cheshire dived from 12,000 ft to 3000 ft through a hail of flak and searchlight, dropping two red spot fires right on the vast marshalling yard. These were immediately backed up by Shannon and Kearns from similar heights. Fawke, meanwhile, had a malfunction and did not release his markers. Fortunately for him, by then the target was clearly visible in any case. Accurate bombing saw the yards heavily damaged, but as they left the area and headed for home, several crews came under fire and Flt Lt John Cooper (in DV394/KC-M) was shot down. Cooper and five others survived to be taken prisoner, but the bomb aimer, Flg Off George Harden, was killed.

Because of the strict fuel limit, Cheshire and the other Mosquito crews had to turn for home straight away, instead of staying over the target as they might otherwise have done. When Fawke approached Manston he was 'shot up inaccurately by an enemy intruder', as Cheshire later recorded in his journal. The CO was then left to land in pitch darkness, as the runway lights were immediately switched off at the Kent airfield following the attack.

Cheshire later considered the Munich mission to be his finest single triumph of the war. Despite the restricted range of his Mosquitos and the heavy defences around the target, the marking was extremely accurate, with more than 90 per cent of the bombs dropped hitting the target. These in turn caused more damage on that one raid than in all the attacks by RAF and US Army Air Force (USAAF) heavy bombers up to that point in the conflict. Cheshire also recorded that 'the spoof raid led by Flt Lt Edward was an unqualified success, and very ably executed, although marred by the fact that they were not permitted to drop bombs'.

On 1 May No 617 Sqn received word that its badge, submitted for approval almost a year before, had finally been approved with the preferred *Apres Moi le Deluge'* motto chosen by the King. The official description of the badge was given as 'On a roundel, a wall in fesse, fractured by three flashes of lightning in pile and issuant from the breach, water proper'.

PREPARING FOR D-DAY

By the spring of 1944, the Allies' intended invasion of the European mainland, codenamed Operation *Overlord*, was in the final planning stages. Round the clock bombing by the RAF and USAAF had seen many of the German supply lines disrupted or destroyed.

Returning from leave on 2 May, Cheshire attended a special pre-invasion planning conference at Bomber Command HQ, where he expected to be told of the important bombing role No 617 Sqn would play. However, to his dismay, he learned instead that the unit would not be required for bombing operations, or even to operate over enemy territory at all. Instead, No 617 Sqn was to mount a diversionary raid over the English Channel, something he initially considered to be 'rather dull', despite acknowledging its tactical worth.

Mosquito DZ521/AZ-M at Woodhall Spa in mid-1944, with its usual No 627 Sqn pilot, Flg Off 'Tommy' Thomson (right). Flt Lt Gerry Fawke flew this particular aircraft to Mailly-le-Camp on 3 May 1944 when No 617 was asked to supply four Mosquito markers. The aircraft was destroyed in a crash near Kings Lynn, in Norfolk, after a No 627 Sqn operation to Karlsruhe on 27 September 1944, with the loss of both crew (*Brian Harris*)

The unit immediately stood down from operations so as to allow it to commence extensive training in preparation for its D-Day mission. However, on 3 May Cheshire, Shannon, Kearns and Fawke were detailed to act as markers in support of a main force operation to bomb a German panzer training camp at Mailly-le-Camp, in France. Cheshire later noted that 'permission was not granted for the rest of the squadron to take any part in the attack'.

Over Mailly, he was again first in and marked well, as did the other Mosquitos, but as he tried to radio the main force controller, Cheshire found that he could not make contact. The controller's wireless had been wrongly tuned, and it was instead receiving an American Forces broadcast! This simple error ultimately proved disastrous, for as crews began circling the target waiting for orders, German fighters pounced. Eventually, the deputy controller took over and the attack proceeded, wiping out the entire panzer division on the ground – but not before 42 of the 346 bombers involved had been shot down by the enemy fighters.

As preparations for the invasion continued, Cheshire received a visit on 9 May from Dr Robert Cockburn of the Telecommunications Research Establishment, who gave him more details about the mission the unit was training for. Operation *Taxable*, as it was codenamed, would require the crews to fly between the British and French coastline with pinpoint accuracy, dropping metal foil strips, known as 'window'. These would in turn confuse the enemy radar into believing that a huge seaborne force was approaching, when in reality the force would be heading for Normandy, further down the coast. To aid navigation, several more aircraft were fitted with H2S (including ED909, one of the original 'Dambusters' that had since been converted to standard configuration and recoded KC-P), as well as other similar radio devices.

Crews continued their training throughout May, mostly flying navigational exercises around the UK that were punctured on occasion by cancellations due to low cloud and bad weather. The Mosquito crews, meanwhile, practiced their dive techniques and air-to-ground firing, Cheshire often being accompanied on these sorties by a different selection of passengers, including Air Commodore Sharpe.

All this was temporarily forgotten on 16 May when No 617 Sqn celebrated the first anniversary of the Dams raid with a party in the Officers' Mess, to which all former members of the squadron who had taken part were invited. Unfortunately, Guy Gibson was unable to attend, but many others did, including several from A V Roe and Vickers, who had worked on the original project. Three days later a dance was held for all ranks, and this time Gibson was present. Indeed, he received a rousing reception as he entered the room. A short while later, he and Cheshire were jointly presented with a cake and, responding to requests for a speech, Gibson climbed onto the table. But he slipped and trod on the cake in the process, following it up immediately with a jocular remark about the dangers of 'icing' (a hazard faced by all crews at high altitude), which just added to the frivolity.

The morning of 5 June brought with it a signal from Bomber Command informing No 617 Sqn that its D-Day operation would be flown later that night. As it was so secret, no further details were included, but these would be revealed to the crews later at a briefing. The invasion of Europe was now just hours away.

Operation *Taxable* would take place in conjunction with Operation *Glimmer*, which was a similar diversionary mission that was to be carried out by No 218 Sqn. It was hoped that the two operations would draw enemy forces northwards, away from the real invasion flotilla that was heading for Normandy. If successful, the 2nd Tactical Air Force would then attack bridges along the route taken by German grounds forces, thus cutting off their means of return back to the Normandy beachhead.

Sixteen Lancasters were detailed to take part in the operation, these aircraft being split into two waves some two hours apart. Each bomber would be fitted with an extra *Gee* set and flare chute, and carry a mixed crew of between 11 and 14, comprising the usual seven, plus an extra pilot, navigator and several others who would despatch the bundles of 'window'.

Each aircraft would fly a straight course towards the French coast for two-and-a-half minutes at a height of 3000 ft and speed of 180 mph, dropping 'window' every 15 seconds along the way. At two miles apart, they would therefore create a 'wall' of window some 16 miles wide. On a given signal they would turn 180 degrees and fly back for two minutes and ten seconds, still dropping 'window', before turning again and repeating the procedure.

By reducing the amount of time the crews spent heading back to the English coast before again approaching France, the Lancasters would create the impression that the 'invading force' was slowly moving forward. Accurate navigation was therefore essential to prevent the illusion from being detected. The dropping of 'window' was not a straightforward task either. The second navigator operated a system of red and green lights that told the operator when to drop. Differing sizes were used, with the larger strips dropped on the run towards the French coast and the smaller ones on the return leg towards the English coast. None were dropped during the turns.

An hour after the first wave began, the second was to approach the area, joining the circuit on the same pattern, but some 500 ft higher. It would take over the duty as the lower aircraft left the area after their final run. The second wave would then begin the same procedure, descending to 3000 ft as they began. To further confuse the enemy radar the Royal Navy also employed radio countermeasures.

Despite the fact that this was not a bombing or marking operation, for the crews involved it was to prove one of the most important, precise and concentrated missions of the whole war. Any deviation from the course, speed or timing, or any mistake in the dropping of the window, could reveal the bluff. Additionally, the aircraft flew without fighter escort in bright moonlight, all the time creeping ever closer to the hostile French coast and the threat of anti-aircraft fire and fighters. It was tiring for all on board, so crews took turns in their duties, periodically handing over to their deputies. It is interesting to note that although Munro and Cheshire flew in the same aircraft, Munro recorded the total flight as having lasted six hours, while Cheshire noted eight-and-a-half.

In the event, Operation *Taxable* was an overwhelming success, with German forces drawn away from Normandy and stretched over a wide area. A measure of both the importance of the operation, and the toll it took on the crews, can be summed up by a comment in the logbook of Sqn Ldr Les Munro, who wrote;

'The creation of a tactical surprise to support the landing of troops on the opening of the second front was the most hazardous, difficult and most dangerous operation ever undertaken in the history of air warfare. It involved flying within at least nine miles of the enemy coast without fighter cover in conditions of bright moonlight and a height of not more than 3000 ft. At this altitude the aircraft was open to attack by the deadliest of all weapons – light flak. Operation believed to be successful.'

This was Munro's 50th operational flight, and it was duly signed off by his squadron commander, who added the comment, 'Certified that Sqn Ldr Munro is still in possession of most of his faculties after completing the operation described by him on this page'.

One of the longest serving crews on No 617 Sqn was that of Sqn Ldr Les Munro, seen here posing next to their regular Lancaster LM482/KC-W in early May 1944 as their prepare to bid farewell to their former bomb aimer Flg Off Jim Clay (back row, second from left), who had ceased his operational flying several weeks before. The rest of the crew continued to fly with a new bomb aimer, completing another eight operations (all in this aircraft), including the D-Day spoof raid Operation *Taxable*, before they too left in mid-June 1944. Standing in the back row, from left to right, are Munro, Clay, Flt Sgt Bill Howarth (mid-upper gunner) and WO Harvey Weeks (rear gunner). In the front row, from left to right, are Flg Off Frank Rumbles (navigator), Flt Sgt Frank Appleby (flight engineer) and Plt Off Reg Pigeon (wireless operator) (*Greg Pigeon*)

TALLBOY

As noted earlier in this volume, at the start of the war Barnes Wallis, designer of the mine used on the Dams raid, had envisaged a streamlined ten-tonne bomb that would bury itself in the earth before exploding, thereby creating an 'earthquake' effect which would shake a target down even if the bomb fell some way away. At the time the project was dropped, as no aircraft was then capable of carrying such a weapon. Wallis instead focused his attention on *Upkeep*. However, with the introduction of the Lancaster, the prospect of developing such a bomb for frontline use lay tantalisingly close.

After satisfactory tests of a 4000-lb trial version of the bomb, a 12,000-lb (six-tonne) example was manufactured with the name of *Tallboy*. Some 21 ft long, it was comprised of a cast steel body containing three fuse pistols and an aluminium tail section. As it fell, the weapon attained a nose-down attitude and started to spin (caused by offset fins on the tail), reaching a maximum rotational velocity of 300 rpm before drilling into the earth, where it would explode. Unlike conventional bombs, it was suspended in the bomb-bay by means of a heavy cast-link 'chain', which was secured with an electrical release unit. On 22 April 1944, Flt Lts David Wilson and John Pryor and Lt 'Nick' Knilans (an American serving with No 617 Sqn) had flown to Boscombe Down to participate in trials with the new weapon, returning to Woodhall Spa two days later.

Just prior to performing Operation *Taxable*, No 617 Sqn had taken possession of the first few *Tallboys*, and only three days later (8 June) the unit was destined to use the weapon for the first time against the Saumur railway tunnel and nearby bridge in the Loire region of France. Destruction of these targets was of vital importance as the rail line that utilised them ran from southwest France up to Normandy, making it a major supply artery for enemy reinforcements to that area.

The aircraft performing this mission took off in the late evening – two Mosquitos (Shannon, flying DZ418/AZ-L borrowed from No 627 Sqn, had to return early with engine failure) and 25 Lancasters, which was the largest number of aircraft put up for any operation by No 617 Sqn to date. Three more Lancasters remained at Woodhall Spa as there was insufficient time available for the groundcrews to prepare them. Nineteen carried *Tallboys*, the rest (including two of the original 'Dambusters', ED909/KC-P and ED933/KC-N) being loaded with 1000-lb bombs. This would prove to be the last time that any of the former 'Dambuster' aircraft would be used in action.

With initial illumination of the target area provided by No 83 Sqn, Cheshire began his marking run just after 0200 hrs, diving from 3000 ft to drop red spot fires at 500 ft on the embankment by the southeastern end of the tunnel mouth. Fawke, in the other Mosquito, dropped his on the northern entrance. The rest of the squadron began to bomb minutes later, several near hits being observed despite smoke quickly obscuring the target. Initial reconnaissance photographs taken

Dr Barnes Wallis of Vickers-Armstrong not only invented the *Upkeep* mine used by No 617 Sqn during the Dams raid, but also the *Tallboy* and *Grandslam* 'earthquake' weapons that the unit so effectively employed. In 1951 he was awarded £10,000 for his scientific and armament developments, which he used to establish the RAF Foundationers Trust at Christ's Hospital, a charitable boarding school in Horsham, West Sussex, at which Wallis had been a former pupil (and later a Governor and Treasurer). His donation was matched by the RAF Benevolent Fund, and it remains in place to this day, providing 'an income for the education of a small number of children in the School at any one time. Consideration for places is given to children of personnel who are serving, or who have served, in the RAF'

Tallboy bomb casings seen on their delivery pallets in the Woodhall Spa bomb dump prior to the fitment of the aluminium tail section. Each weapon was fitted with three fuse pistols, installed in the rear end plate (seen to the left), which was bolted to the bomb casing (*Vic Gill*)

the next morning showed that the target had been severely damaged, with each end of the tunnel blocked, the hillside above it blown away and the nearby bridge and rail line put out of action. The squadron was in high sprits, and Wallis' theories on earthquake weapons were seemingly proved.

The official report on the attack written some ten months later painted a different picture, however. Although the results of *Tallboy* were indeed impressive, an operation carried out by the USAAF two weeks later, on 22 June, was found to have caused a similar blockage at the mouth of the tunnel using just 1000-lb bombs. The main devastation (the huge explosion that obliterated the centre of the tunnel and destroyed the hillside above it) was almost certainly aided by the fact that a munitions train was in the tunnel at the time, and seemingly right underneath a direct *Tallboy* hit.

Mission planners in Bomber Command argued, therefore, that if the objective was to merely block the tunnel, then *Tallboy* might not be 'the most profitable weapon, since an effective block was caused by a

Armourers preparing to bolt the lightweight aluminium tail section to a *Tallboy*. Twelve small bolts held the tail in place, with an aluminium cowling between the two to help keep the streamlined aerodynamic shape (*Ken Parkin*)

A complete *Tallboy* is carefully winched onto a special bomb trolley. The fins on the tail section were slightly offset by five degrees, giving the weapon a right-hand spin as it fell, before drilling into the earth and exploding (*Beck Parsons*)

chance hit by a much smaller bomb'. Although some bombs had exploded under the surface as intended (leaving craters some 76 ft wide), analysis concluded that most of the weapons were fitted with fuses whose delay was so short that the bombs exploded almost immediately upon hitting the ground, which in turn left the tunnel walls largely intact.

Meanwhile, the Germans worked night and day to clear the rubble, and they had the tunnel back in use within three weeks. They did, however, leave some debris behind in order to give the impression that the tunnel was still out of action when viewed from the air by Allied reconnaissance aircraft.

Poor weather curtailed most flying over the next few days. The six H2S crews had been ordered to return to their original squadrons on 9 June, but even they were delayed by a day because of the heavy rain. Finally, on the 14th, the weather broke long enough for No 617 Sqn to fly to Le Havre, in France, to bomb the E-boat pens. Putting these heavily reinforced concrete structures out of action was essential in removing the German naval threat to Allied ships crossing the Channel in support of the invasion force, which was now moving inland. The unit's aircraft would again be carrying *Tallboys* as part of a force of more than 220 aircraft, and operating in daylight for the first time in over a year.

Tallboys sit on their special trolleys in the bomb dump at RAF Bardney, home to No 9 Sqn, which was the only other squadron to use the weapon. Nos 617 and 9 Sqns flew several operations together with *Tallboys*. Unlike conventional bombs, which were winched up into the aircraft from above, the *Tallboy* was raised up from the trolley below using four winches, one on each corner of the trolley

Taking off in the early evening, the bombers were escorted by a squadron of Spitfires, although in the event no enemy fighters were encountered. The flak, however, was intense, and several aircraft were damaged. Cheshire's marking was

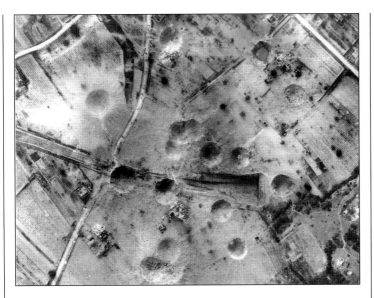

The southern entrance of the Saumar Railway Tunnel, photographed the morning after the attack on 8-9 June 1944. This was the first time the 12,000-lb *Tallboy* bomb was used operationally, and the accuracy can be seen by the two craters left on the railway tracks themselves, and a direct hit on the roof of the tunnel. Fifteen more craters can be counted within 220 yards of the tunnel (*IWM Neg No HU92978*)

so accurate that he decided that neither reserve marker was required, instructing them instead to observe the bombing, which was well concentrated around the aiming point. Although some ordnance from the main force fell in the town, most of the damage inflicted on the target appears to have been done by No 617 Sqn's bombs, one of which went straight through the 16-ft thick reinforced concrete roof of one of the pens and exploded inside. The E-boat threat at Le Havre had gone.

The following evening, a force of almost 300 aircraft drawn from Nos 1, 4, 5, 6 and 8 Groups attacked the E-boat pens at Boulogne in what was hoped would be a repeat of the Le Havre operation. Thick cloud and heavy flak was encountered over the target, however, and several aircraft were hit, not least DV403/KC-G, flown by Flg Off Mac Hamilton, which had one of its bomb-bay doors blown off. The aircraft subsequently made a hasty landing at an emergency airstrip in southern England so that bomb aimer Flg Off Bob Duck could have almost 30 pieces of shrapnel removed from his thigh.

When No 617 Sqn bombed the E-boat pens at Le Havre on 14 June 1944, one *Tallboy* pierced the 16-ft reinforced concrete roof before exploding inside. The resulting shockwave was sufficient to collapse the rest (*IWM Neg No CL1208*)

Although Cheshire was flying as the only marker that night, the force caused great destruction in the area, despite only a few No 617 Sqn aircraft delivering their ordnance. Indeed, as the cloud increased, Cheshire ordered ten of his Lancasters back to Woodhall Spa with their *Tallboys* still aboard.

STEPPING UP THE V-WEAPON CAMPAIGN

Despite Bomber Command mounting several operations against V-weapon construction sites in late 1943, the threat remained. In the early summer of 1944, London and the southeast of England began to feel the full effect of the V1 'flying bomb' campaign, with weapons raining down indiscriminately, killing hundreds of civilians and causing widespread destruction. Launched from France and flying at high speed, the V1s initially appeared to be unstoppable. Worse was to follow when the V1 was replaced by the more powerful V2 – a streamlined rocket that was launched into the stratosphere, where it attained supersonic speeds, before falling back to earth and causing even greater devastation than the V1.

Intelligence received from France during the spring and early summer of 1944 had pinpointed the location of a number of V-weapon factories and launch sites, and these were treated as top priority targets by Bomber Command.

With poor weather delaying operations for several days, groundcrews set about repairing the aircraft damaged over Boulogne. When conditions finally cleared on the 19th (only six days after the first V1 had fallen on London), orders were received to attack the flying bomb factories at Watten, in France. Although Flt Lt 'Kit' Howard returned early after a problem in ED763/KC-D, 17 Lancasters and two Mosquitos, supported by another nine bombers from No 8 Group, attacked the site with only partial success after cloud obscured the aiming point.

A similar operation to Wizernes, in France, the following day was aborted as the formation approached the target, again because of heavy cloud. Twice more, on the 21st and 22nd, the same target was detailed for attack but aborted because of the weather.

Finally, on 24 June, two Mosquitos and 16 Lancasters succeeded in reaching Wizernes and bombing on markers dropped by Fawke (as Cheshire had a fault and was unable to release his). Although smoke from the bomb bursts began to drift across the target, several good hits

Mosquito DZ547/AZ-E of No 627 Sqn, which Flt Lt Gerry Fawke flew on the abortive raid to Wizernes on 20 June 1944. It is seen here at Woodhall Spa being prepared for an operation. Remaining with the unit for the rest of the war, it was finally struck off charge in October 1946 (*Brian Harris*)

Flt Lt Shannon flew DZ637/AZ-O on the 20 June 1944 operation, this aircraft being another Mosquito borrowed from No 627 Sqn. A fighter-bomber version fitted with bulged bomb-bay doors to enable it to carry a 4000-lb 'Cookie', it had previously flown with No 692 Sqn. Whilst still with No 627 Sqn, it was lost with its crew during an operation to Berlin on 2 February 1945 (*IWM Neg No CH12624*)

No 617 Sqn borrowed three Mosquitos for the next operation, again to Wizernes, on 22 June 1944. Flt Lt Gerry Fawke flew DZ525/AZ-S, but once again poor weather over the target meant that it too was aborted. The aircraft survived the war and was struck off charge on 21 September 1945 (*Brian Harris*)

were seen and bombing was well concentrated around the aiming point. However, tragedy struck when Flt Lt John Edward's aircraft (DV403/KC-G) was hit by flak as he began his run in. The bomber's port wing and two engines burst into flames and flight engineer Flg Off Les King was killed by shrapnel. Unable to dowse the flames, Edward ordered the crew to bail out, but of the eight on board only three survived – Plt Off Tom Price of Flg Off Bill Carey's crew was aboard as an extra gunner. This was the first crew lost by No 617 Sqn in two months.

Flt Lt John Edward (second from right) and his crew after carrying out a practice dinghy drill. They were posted to No 617 Sqn in mid-February 1944, but their luck ran out during the third attempt to bomb Wizernes on 24 June that year. Carrying an extra gunner, they were hit by flak as they ran into the target, and although most of the crew managed to bail out, only three survived (*Gerry Hobbs*)

By the spring of 1944, No 54 Base at RAF Coningsby was supplying 'Master Bombers' for No 5 Group operations. Personnel charged with performing this role controlled all aspects of the mission over the target. The first 'Master Bomber' had been Wg Cdr Gibson during the Dams raid, followed by Wg Cdr Cheshire, who had greatly expanded the role during his time as CO of No 617 Sqn.

Although Cheshire's use of the Mosquito had been very successful, he realised that a faster and more agile aircraft was needed when marking during daylight operations, and this lead to investigations into what other types might be suitable. Although trials were conducted with the American P-38 Lightning, which was much favoured thanks to its twin engines and long range, Cheshire himself had been giving the matter some thought, and he was interested in another fighter type.

At the end of March, Woodhall Spa had received a visit from the USAAF Gens Carl Spaatz and James Doolittle, and together with Cheshire they had spoken at great length about marking techniques, the *Tallboy* weapons and bombing operations in general. Cheshire had mentioned his thoughts on a smaller aircraft for marking, and it is probable that the merits of the American P-51 Mustang were discussed, or at least mentioned, in this role. The Mustang had originally been built to fulfil a British fighter requirement, and once fitted with a Rolls-Royce Merlin engine, it quickly proved itself to be the best Allied long-range piston-engined escort fighter of the war. Fast and agile at all altitudes, it was just the type of thing Cheshire was looking for.

After some enquiries, the No 617 Sqn CO was eventually allocated two brand new Mustang IIIs (HB825 and HB839) from a batch that had already been allocated to the RAF under the lend-lease scheme. Arriving at Woodhall Spa on 21 June 1944 still in their packing crates, they were taken into a hanger and reassembled. At the same time, attachment points were fixed under each wing to carry the ordnance for marking.

Cheshire was keen to use one of his new machines operationally as soon as possible, and groundcrews managed to get HB839 rebuilt in time for its participation in No 617 Sqn's next mission on 25 June. The unit was to attack a 'flying bomb' storage depot at Siracourt, in

Wg Cdr Cheshire (left) greets Gen Carl Spaatz of the USAAF at the start of the latter's visit to Woodhall Spa on 31 March 1944. Also seen in the photograph, from left to right, is Grp Capt Monty Philpott (Station Commander), AVM Cochrane (No 5 Group commander) and (right) Gen James Doolittle. It was during this visit that Cheshire first discussed the merits of using the American P-51 Mustang aircraft in the target marking role (*Sir Leonard Cheshire*)

Cheshire is seen at the controls of Mustang III HB839 during the daylight raid to Mimoyecques on 6 July 1944 – his last operation with No 617 Sqn. This aircraft was one of two Mustang IIIs assigned to the unit until early October 1944. It later served with Nos 541 and 309 Sqns, before being struck off charge in March 1947 (*Paul Clark*)

France. With the reassembly completed only a few hours before the unit was to depart on the operation, Cheshire had no time for a practice flight in the fighter. Therefore, come the morning of the mission, with most of the squadron already airborne, the CO climbed into the cockpit of the Mustang III and started the engine. Incredibly, he then took off on what was not only the aircraft's initial air-test after reassembly, but also its first operational flight. To complete this series of 'firsts', this was also Cheshire's maiden flight in a Mustang!

For the first time in years the legendary bomber pilot was also flying alone, navigating for himself. However, he reached the target without incident and circled at 3000 ft, before diving down to 500 ft, where he dropped two red flares, which were backed up by Shannon and Fawke in their Mosquitos. The squadron bombed well and obtained three direct *Tallboy* hits, which although causing only minor damage overall, effectively put the complex out of action. With a final look at the target, Cheshire turned the Mustang for home. All he had to do now was try and land the unfamiliar aircraft!

Cheshire had surpassed himself on 25 June. The pioneering Mustang flight had demonstrated what a supreme pilot and marker he was, and the follow-up marking and bombing by the rest of the crews had shown exactly what was now being achieved.

Poor weather saw operations cancelled several times over the last week of June and into the first week of July, but on the 4th it did break long enough for 17 Lancasters, a Mosquito and Cheshire, once again in the Mustang, to attack the V-weapon storage site at Creil, near Paris. The target was well protected and the approach hazardous, being housed in natural chalk caves. However, in the single-seater, Cheshire had little trouble marking the target, diving to 800 ft and dropping two red target spot fires so accurately that Fawke in the Mosquito was not required to mark at all. The follow-up bombing was very successful, despite five crews returning (for a variety of reasons) with their loads still aboard.

After only a day's respite, No 617 Sqn was detailed to bomb the V-weapon site at Mimoyecques, in France, on 6 July – one of five targets attacked by a force totalling 550+ aircraft. Mimoyecques held a new and potentially more devastating V-weapon in the form of the V3 'Supergun'. Effectively a smooth-bore barrel some 130 metres long, it was built into a hillside. The weapon featured a number of separate chambers along its length containing solid fuel boosters, which would detonate in series as a

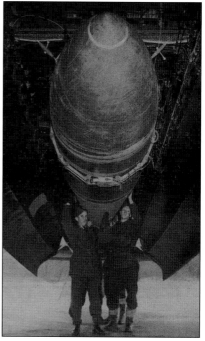

Above

One of a series of official photographs taken showing ED763/KC-D being prepared for its 24th operation – to Mimoyecques – on 6 July 1944 with Flt Lt 'Kit' Howard and his crew aboard. ED763 was one of the initial ten Lancasters assigned to No 617 Sqn (and coded AJ-D) when it was formed in March 1943, and the bomber duly became the unit's longest serving aircraft. It survived the war only to be struck off charge on 14 May 1945 and scrapped (*Ken Parkins*)

Above right

An unusual view of a *Tallboy* in the bomb-bay of a Lancaster. The release unit at the bottom of the bomb, which could be opened either manually or electronically, secures the linked 'chain' that holds the weapon in place. The double curvature bulged bomb-bay doors, fitted to enable the *Tallboy* and 12,000-lb HC bombs to be carried internally by the Lancaster, are clearly visible (*Sport & General*)

shell was fired, increasing its velocity to about 3300 ft per second as it finally left the barrel and headed towards London. The complex was designed to hold 25 guns at each of its two locations, with the barrels arranged in five rows of five. Covering the complex at ground level was a concrete slab that was 98 ft in width and 18 ft thick, with robust steel doors protecting the individual gun ports. Over the previous few months the site had already been bombed six times by the USAAF and once by the RAF, but without any great success.

No 617 Sqn got airborne just after noon, with Cheshire leading again in the Mustang. He marked with two red spot fires before climbing to observe as the crews began to release their *Tallboys*. Three near-misses and one direct hit on the corner of the concrete slab were enough to cause the collapse of one of the gun shafts and some of the underground tunnels, so Cheshire ordered the remaining crews back to base without bombing.

The earthquake effect of the *Tallboys* had caused such damage that the Germans eventually decided to cease building at this site. However, as this was unknown to the Allies at the time, the USAAF mounted two further raids, the second of which was a bizarre operation using a radio-controlled B-24 Liberator packed with explosives under the codename Project *Anvil*. The pilot of the aircraft was Lt Joseph Kennedy, elder brother of the future president of the United States. Before he was able to set the B-24 on course and bail out, the Liberator exploded, killing both Kennedy and his engineer. The Canadian 3rd Infantry Division eventually captured Mimoyecques on 5 September 1944, the site having never been made operational by the Germans.

The Mimoycques raid had been Cheshire's 100th operational flight, and it saw the completion of his fourth tour – an incredible achievement. The following morning he was taken aside by Cochrane, who told him that he had done enough, and was therefore being taken off operations. Despite the protests Cochrane would not be swayed. At the same time the three flight commanders, Les Munro, David Shannon and Joe McCarthy, were also to be rested. They were the last of the original pilots still flying with the squadron, and had each been on continuous operations for more than two years.

Various messages of congratulations filtered in over the next few days, and a party was arranged for the leavers at the Petwood Hotel, which had been procured by the RAF for use as an Officers' Mess for Woodhall Spa. Although Cheshire had been an inspirational pilot and leader, instilling confidence in all ranks within the squadron, it was obvious that he could not continue as commanding officer indefinitely, and the choice to replace him had actually been made several weeks previously. At the beginning of June 1944, Cochrane had written to Harris remarking that the 'old guard' of No 617 Sqn was finally due to be rested from operations, and as such he had 'earmarked Tait' to succeed Cheshire.

Wg Cdr James Brian Tait (known throughout the RAF as 'Willie' Tait) was a 27-year-old pre-war officer who had graduated from the RAF College at Cranwell in 1936. He was posted to Whitley-equipped No 51 Sqn in early 1940, and had become its commanding officer by year's end. Tait later received both a DFC then a DSO whilst with this unit. He subsequently moved to No 35 Sqn and flew the Halifax as a flight commander, where he received a second DSO and a MiD, before being posted to No 22 Operational Training Unit (OTU) as an instructor in early 1942. Whilst with the latter, Tait managed to fly on all three 'Thousand Bomber' raids that were mounted that spring, one of which he completed on just three engines after a failure during the outward flight.

In April 1942 Tait assumed command of Halifax-equipped No 10 Sqn for a short time, after which he led No 78 Sqn (again flying the Halifax) for almost two years, gaining another MiD. He was then made Operations Officer at RAF Waddington. Like the spell at No 22 OTU, the Waddington posting did not require Tait to fly on operations, but he still did, often with the more junior crews. His last appointment before taking command of No 617 Sqn was an official return to operations as a 'Master Bomber' with No 5 Group. By the time he

Les Munro, seen here on the rear terrace of the Petwood Hotel at Woodhall Spa, was one of the original pilots posted to No 617 Sqn. On his way to the Sorpe Dam during the unit's first operation, his bomber was hit by flak, necessitating an early return home. Munro remained with the squadron for over a year, finally standing down from operations in mid-July 1944 (*Les Munro*)

Far left
American Joe McCarthy, seen here in the cockpit of EE148/KC-U *UNCLE CHUCK CHUCK* in July 1943, flew three trips in this bomber between 15 and 29 July 1943. The aircraft was then transferred to No 626 Sqn, with whom it was lost with its crew on an operation to Mailly-le-Camp on 4 May 1944 (*Dave Rodger*)

Left
Flt Lt David Shannon poses outside the gates of Buckingham Palace after collecting his second DSO in March 1945. By the time he left No 617 Sqn at the end of July 1944, he had completed almost 70 operations. Shannon finished the war as the most highly decorated Australian airman, with two DSOs and two DFCs (*J Shannon*)

arrived at Woodhall Spa to take over from Cheshire, Tait had completed more than three operational tours, and although quiet and shy by nature, was a strong commander who led from the front.

The two men were already firm friends, Cheshire having been CO of No 35 Sqn when Tait had joined, and they later shared an airfield – Linton-on-Ouse – when in command of Nos 76 and 78 Sqns respectively. Likeminded, they frequently discussed tactics, operations and squadron matters.

On 2 June 1944 Cheshire had taken Tait up for his first Mosquito flight to demonstrate the dive-bombing and air firing techniques that he was employing on operations at the time, and a few days later Tait took one up himself. Cheshire formerly handed over command of No 617 Sqn on 12 July, signing the 'receipt', which Tait pasted into his logbook. Within a few days Cheshire had left for the RAF College at Cranwell, where he was to attend a Senior Commander's course.

With the magnificent work done by Cheshire to improve bombing and marking techniques, as well as accuracy (aside from his own operational flying), an appropriate award was discussed. Unknown to him, Woodhall Spa's station commander, Grp Capt Monty Philpott, had written to Cochrane recommending him for a third bar to his DSO, but as this moved up the chain of command the award changed to a VC, which was officially announced on 9 September 1944. Uniquely, Cheshire received the decoration not for a single act of bravery, as was the norm, but for a sustained campaign of bombing operations and the development of marking techniques. This was the second VC awarded to No 617 Sqn, which was still only 16 months old.

The day after Tait took command the squadron was detailed for operations again, but these were subsequently cancelled, as they were on 16 July. Indeed, it was not until the 17th that Tait had his first opportunity to lead his new charges into battle, the target being the V-weapons factories at Wizernes once again. A Mustang III (being flown operationally by Tait for the first time), 16 Lancasters and a Mosquito was No 617 Sqn's contribution to a force of more than 130 aircraft that

Wg Cdr James 'Willie' Tait replaced Cheshire as CO of No 617 Sqn in July 1944. Highly experienced, holder of two DSOs, a DFC and two MiDs, he was flying as a Master Bomber within No 5 Group when he received orders to No 617 Sqn. Tait remained in the RAF after the war, retiring in 1964 with the rank of group captain, having served as Aide de Camp to Her Majesty the Queen (*Tait Family*)

The V2 rocket factory and launch site at Wizernes, in France, is seen here just before the fourth attack by No 617 Sqn on 17 July 1944. The enormous one million ton concrete dome covering the complex can be clearly seen. This operation was the first for new CO, Wg Cdr Tait, and the most successful on this target, with much of the hillside under the dome collapsing, sealing many of the entrance tunnels (*IWM Neg No C4509*)

Seen from the cockpit of a neighbouring aircraft, Mosquito DZ484/AZ-G of No 627 Sqn had first been used by No 617 Sqn on the Le Havre raid of 14 June 1944. The unit borrowed it again on 20 July, when CO 'Willie' Tait took it to Wizernes for the fifth, and final, attack on the target by No 617 Sqn. Like a number of previous attempts, the operation was ultimately aborted because of poor weather (*Brian Harris*)

attacked three sites in all, taking off just before lunch. They arrived over the target an hour later, Tait releasing red spot fires after diving down to 500 ft, backed up by Fawke 90 seconds later. Several bombs fell on the nearby rail lines and tunnels, while many buildings were damaged when a landslide was caused by the earthquake effect of the ordnance.

Despite the success of this mission, a return was detailed for the night of 20/21 July, when several No 627 Sqn Mosquitos accompanied them. As they neared the target, cloud and haze began to mount, which made marking and aiming so difficult that Tait ordered the aircraft back to base without bombing.

With the now-familiar cycle of operations scheduled and cancelled due to weather, it was not until 25 July that 16 Lancasters took off to bomb the V-weapon store at Watten with outstanding results. As the target was clearly visible in the mid-morning light, no markers were necessary, although the flak was extremely heavy and several aircraft were hit as they made their runs. Flg Off Don Cheney (in DV393/KC-T) was one, momentarily losing control before jettisoning his *Tallboy* short of the target. In the confusion, mid-upper gunner Flt Sgt Arthur McRostie bailed out, having convinced himself that a lack of answers to his calls meant that the aircraft was going down. In reality, the intercom had simply failed.

No 617 Sqn's next mission came on the last day of July, when it flew to Rilly la Montagne, in France, to bomb a rail tunnel that was being used to store V1s and flying bomb components. Part of a force of more than 100 aircraft, Tait led in a Mosquito for the first time, with a second machine flown by Flg Off Warren Duffy – the latter was newly converted to the type. Neither pilot found that their marking was required due to clear weather conditions, so they observed the bombing instead. This proved to be very accurate, sealing both ends of the tunnel and damaging many of the surrounding rail lines and approach roads.

As the unit returned to Woodhall Spa, it was realised that Flt Lt Bill Reid was missing. Having just completed his run over the target, his Lancaster (ME557/KC-S) was hit by two bombs falling from another aircraft above. The first severed the two port engines and the other sliced through the fuselage and control rods. As the aircraft began to plunge earthwards, breaking up as it turned over, Reid and his wireless operator, Flg Off David Luker, were thrown clear. The rest of the crew remained trapped inside ME557, and they perished when it hit the ground.

Undertaking his second tour, Reid had been awarded a VC for an operation in November 1943 with No 61 Sqn when, injured and nursing

THUMPER III was Flt Lt Bob Knights'
DV385/KC-A, which is seen here
after completing its 35th trip, to
Watten, on 25 July 1944. The
tally includes a small letter 'D'
(for Operation Taxable) on the
23rd bomb, and, interestingly, a
swastika on the 32nd (6 July 1944
to Mimoyecques), denoting the
successful downing of an enemy
fighter, although no mention of
the action is recorded in squadron
records. Having later been recoded
KC-V, DV385 was finally retired
in April 1945, having flown 51
operations. It was struck off
charge in early November 1946
(Bob Knights)

a damaged Lancaster, he had pressed on to the target and bombed it, before turning for home. He had joined No 617 Sqn in February 1944, and the unit later received word that both he and Luker were safe as prisoners of war.

1 August saw No 617 Sqn attempt to attack a V-weapon factory at Siracourt, in France, but crews were recalled before managing to drop their bombs because of heavy fog across the target area. Similar conditions resulted in only partial success three days later when the unit attacked a rail bridge at Etaples, again in France. Post-raid photographs revealed that although their ordnance had detonated close to the target, no severe damage had been done and the bridge still stood. They had been carrying 1000-lb bombs on this occasion.

Four days later, when detailed to bomb the submarine pens at Brest, the squadron made sure that its aircraft were armed with *Tallboys* instead. The pens were clearly visible in the mid-morning light, and several direct hits were observed. However, one disadvantage of using the SABS was the need for crews to fly straight and level for several minutes in the target area. This was a dangerous thing to do in daylight, as Don Cheney's JB139/KC-V *Dark Victor* found out when it suffered a direct hit. As his *Tallboy* fell away and he banked to port, Cheney realised that both his navigator (Plt Off Roy Welch) and wireless operator (Flt Sgt Reg Pool) had been seriously wounded.

With the aircraft becoming hard to control, Cheney gave the order to bail out – all seven men landed in the sea. Despite being quickly rescued by French fishermen, Welch and Pool did not survive, while rear gunner Plt Off Noel Wait is believed to have drowned after becoming entangled in his parachute. As he swam ashore, bomb aimer Flt Sgt Len Curtis found several German soldiers waiting for him, and he too become a PoW until liberated by American troops later that year. The rest of the crew were safely picked up and turned over to US forces, arriving back in the UK several months later. Cheney himself was back by 4 September, however.

On 6 August No 617 Sqn was briefed to attack the U-boat pens at Lorient, in France. Despite a successful attack through very heavy flak, No 5 Group ordered them to return the following evening to complete the job, bombing those pens that remained. However, the day started badly with an event that cast a dark shadow over the whole squadron. During the morning Flg Off Duffy took off to fly a practice marking exercise over the Wainfleet range in a Mosquito, taking Flg Off Phil Ingleby with him. As he completed his third run Duffy pulled up and climbed, but the starboard engine failed, followed immediately by the collapse of the wing. The crew stood no chance of escape as the aircraft broke up in mid-air, and both men were killed when it crashed a few moments later.

Duffy was immensely popular. He had been told only the previous evening that his operational flying was over, and that within a few days he would be leaving No 617 Sqn to return to his native Canada. Later that day came notice of Duffy's promotion to flight lieutenant and the award of a DFC, making his untimely death even more poignant. It has been speculated that the aircraft they were flying (NT202/N) was the same Mosquito that Cheshire had taken on the Munich raid on 24 April, and that the stresses caused by the severe dive during the operation were possibly a contributing factor in the crash. However, the aircraft Cheshire flew on that mission was NS993/N.

Phil Ingleby, who was usually navigator to Flg Off Geoff Stout, was buried in the cemetery at Coningsby on 10 August, while Duffy was laid to rest in the regional cemetery at Harrogate the following day.

It was with heavy hearts, therefore, that the rest of No 617 Sqn took off for Lorient that evening, but as they neared the target a recall notice was received. US troops were believed to be on the outskirts of the town and preparing to advance. Operations to quell the U-boat threat continued, however, with raids on the pens at La Pallice, in France, on the 9th and 11th. The first operation, using *Tallboys*, was very successful, but the other (with crews carrying 2000-lb armour piercing bombs) was less so.

By this time almost all of No 617 Sqn's operations were being carried out in daylight, diminishing the need for marking, as the targets were usually easily visible. As a result, Tait dispensed with the Mustangs and redeployed the Mosquito crews as airborne reconnaissance assets over the target area. Although there is no record of the second Mustang III (HB825) having ever being flown whilst with No 617 Sqn, both it and the first example (HB839) were sent to No 38 MU on 2 October 1944, from where they were issued to Nos 64 and 541 Sqns respectively.

There was no respite from the raids against enemy shipping and submarines over the next week, with three more trips scheduled to Brest. The first of these, on 12 August, saw Tait revert to a Lancaster (DV380/KC-P) for the first time, carrying a 12,000-lb *Tallboy* that he

Nose art on Don Cheney's Lancaster JB139/KC-V *DARK VICTOR,* which the crew were flying when shot down over Brest on 5 August 1944. Cheney, Jim Rosher, Len Curtis and Ken Porter (who had replaced McRostie) survived, making it back to the UK before the end of the year. Roy Welch, Reg Pool and Noel Wait were not so lucky (*Don Cheney*)

PD238/KC-H joined No 617 Sqn at the end of July 1944, flying its first operation, to the U-boat pens at Lorient, on 6 August in the hands of Flg Off Bill Carey and his crew. The bomber is seen here still carrying plain red code letters, which were changed to red with a yellow outline within weeks of this photograph being taken. PD238 later became the regular aircraft of the A Flight commander Sqn Ldr John Cockshott, and it was finally written off in a crash in November 1945 (*John Cockshott*)

dropped very close to the aiming point. The return mission on the 13th saw the force split, with some crews carrying *Tallboys* to destroy the pens, while the rest attacked the veteran French warship *Gueydon* at its mooring with 1000-lb bombs so as to prevent it being sunk by the Germans in the mouth of Brest harbour, in turn blocking its use by the Allies. Although both targets were hit, *Gueydon* remained afloat, and so the unit returned on the 14th with 2000-lb armour piercing bombs, which left both it and the warship *Clementau* sunk at their moorings.

No 617 Sqn did not escape unscathed on the latter date, however, with intense flak damaging several aircraft. Flt Lt John Pryor' LM485/KC-N was hit as it approached the target, shrapnel smashing the bomber's compass and hitting the throat of bomb aimer Flg Off Cecil Pesme, killing him instantly. Regaining control, Pryor jettisoned his bomb load and returned to base without further incident. Flak also injured pilot Flg Off 'Bunny' Lee over the target, his ankle wound forcing him to make an emergency landing at RAF Beaulieu.

On 16 August the squadron returned to La Pallice, but not a single bomb was dropped because of heavy cloud covering the target area. After a postponement the following day, the unit tried again on the 18th – a mix of *Tallboys* and 2000-lb bombs caused considerable damage.

With operations being carried out almost every day for a week, it was perhaps a blessing for the crews that the weather then closed in, leaving them effectively grounded for six full days. Indeed, they did not operate again until the 24th, when eight crews attacked the E-boat pens at Ijmuiden, in Holland, to help counter the threat posed by the fast surface torpedo boats. Almost no resistance was encountered from the ground or in the air, and several direct hits caused the reinforced concrete roof to partially collapse.

Only one other operation was carried out before the end of the month, on the 27th, when 12 crews (accompanied by a similar number from No 9 Sqn) attacked ships in Brest harbour. There was good news that day too, as word finally reached the unit that Flt Sgt McRostie, the gunner in Don Cheney's crew who had bailed out by mistake during the Watten raid on 25 July, was safe and well as a PoW.

Flg Off Don Cheney with the crew he brought with him from No 630 Sqn in mid-February 1944. In the back row, from left to right, are Flt Sgts Reg Pool (wireless operator) and Jim Rosher (flight engineer), Plt Off Noel Wait (rear gunner) and Flt Sgt Arthur McRostie. In the front row, from left to right, are Plt Off Roy Welch (navigator), Flt Lt Don Cheney (pilot) and and Flt Sgt Len Curtis (bomb aimer). On the operation to Watten on 25 July 1944, McRostie mistakenly bailed out of their aircraft (Lancaster DV393/KC-T) after thinking that it was about to crash, although he survived to become a PoW (*Don Cheney*)

'SHIPBUSTING'

An ever-present threat to Britain throughout the war was the German Kriegsmarine, which constantly prowled the vital supply routes searching for prey in an attempt to literally starve the UK of war supplies, food and other essential goods. The feared battleship *Bismarck* had been sunk by the Royal Navy after a fierce battle in May 1941, but its sister-ship the *Tirpitz* continued to be a worry to the British Admiralty.

Completed in March 1941, the vessel commenced trials in the Baltic Sea before sailing up to Norway, where Hitler intended for it be used to defend the Norwegian coast against a possible invasion by the Allies. Always fearful that the ship might make for the open water, the British had attacked *Tirpitz* several times, initially employing RAF Halifaxs and then Royal Navy midget submarines. The Fleet Air Arm had also mounted a series of attacks with Albacore aircraft, but despite suffering minor damage and casualties amongst its crew, the vessel remained afloat, and a very real threat to shipping in the Atlantic and elsewhere.

The *Tirpitz* problem then fell once more in the lap of RAF Bomber Command, and more specifically No 5 Group, who, with its specialist squadrons, weapons and equipment, was asked to explore ways in which to attack the battleship. Although the choice of units to carry out this mission was predictable, other problems arose, such as the best weapon to use, what defences might be encountered and, of course, the weather. It was eventually decided to use both *Tallboys* and *Johnny Walker* mines, the latter being a weapon that would sink once dropped into water, moving both forwards and sideways, before rising and exploding in contact with anything it touched. If it hit nothing the pattern was repeated.

However, *Tirpitz* lay out of range of British aircraft, even when the latter used the most northerly base in the British Isles. So after much discussion, it was decided that the bombers would fly up to a base in Scotland to refuel, before making their way to the USSR, from where the attack would be mounted. Afterwards, they could regroup and refuel back in the USSR, before returning to Britain. Possible cloud cover over the target and the defences around the ship would have to be assessed nearer the time.

During the first week of September 1944, crews from No 617 Sqn prepared themselves for this operation by flying around the UK to determine the Lancaster's maximum range with a full fuel and bomb load aboard, while Tait went over to see the commanding officer of No 9 Sqn at Bardney, as this unit would be operating alongside No 617 Sqn during the attack.

On 8 September, Cochrane brought crews from both squadrons together so as to brief them on the operation that they were to about to undertake. They would first fly up to RAF Lossiemouth and then out over the cold, unforgiving North Sea, where they would eventually land at Yagodnik, 20 miles from Archangel, in the USSR. All aircraft would be carrying *Tallboys*, although No 9 Sqn would be using the Mk XIV

Sqn Ldr Drew Wyness's Lancaster ME559/KC-Y at Kegostrov on 11 September 1944 after the flight to the USSR for the first attempt on the battleship *Tirpitz*. The aircraft was so badly damaged when Wyness attempted to land that it was left behind when No 617 Sqn returned to the UK. The Russians later repaired the badly damaged nose and turret, replacing them with a large Perspex cover, before allocating the aircraft to their own 16th Transport Flight of the White Sea Navy. It ended its days as a ground instructional airframe with the Russian Aviation Technical College at Riga (*Harry Humphries*)

Accommodation for almost 200 men during their stay in Russia was the old steamboat *Ivan Kalyev*, moored on the River Dvina. Despite the welcome banner, the Russians were not expecting so many guests, and conditions were extremely overcrowded. All those on board were plagued by bed bugs for most of their stay (*Bob Knights*)

The Russians were reluctant to allow any photography by the RAF aircrews during their stay, so this shot of an engine change had to be taken from inside the rear door of a Lancaster, possibly DV391/KC-O – the mount of Flt Lt Bob Knights' crew (*Bob Knights*)

bombsight, as its crews were not familiar with the SABS used by No 617 Sqn. Two No 511 Sqn Liberators would accompany them, carrying spares (including an engine and undercarriage leg), tools, tinned food, groundcrew and the Woodhall Spa Medical Officer, Flt Lt Bob Mathews.

Three days after the initial briefing, 20 aircraft from No 617 Sqn took off and flew to Scotland, before heading for the USSR. To reduce the weight and help increase range, all the Lancasters had their mid-upper turrets removed, the gunner transferring to the front turret. The flights were long, averaging around 11 hours, before Yagodnik came into view. But by this time the weather was bad, with low mist making visibility so poor that some crews had extreme difficulty even finding the airfield. Flg Off Ian Ross searched for two hours before spotting a wooden planked road upon which he attempted a landing. Other crews landed on nearby airstrips, while another two, almost out of fuel, belly-landed in the marshes surrounding the area. Amazingly, no one reported any casualties, and soon the RAF groundcrews, aided by the Russians, set to work on repairing all but two of the Lancasters – this was done in just 48 hours.

As the aircraft were being worked on, the aircrews inspected their quarters. This took the form of the old steamship *Ivan Kalyev*, moored on the River Dvina. It housed 196 officers and senior NCOs, with a further 126 in nearby huts. However, the Russians had not expected so many aircrew, and there was gross overcrowding. Those on board the

A line-up of No 9 Sqn Lancasters on the airfield at Yagodnik, in front of some from No 617 Sqn, before the first attempt on the *Tirpitz* on 12 September 1944. Although the airfield looks flat, the weather was appalling as they arrived, and several aircraft from both units were damaged or written off as they landed there or in surrounding areas (*Mac Hamilton*)

steamer were also plagued by an infestation of bedbugs for most of the first two days. Although the facilities were generally clean, the latrines were considered so poor that the Medical Officer noted in his report, 'these were so disgusting and nauseating that there is little to be gained by detailed descriptions'!

With the aircraft finally repaired and the weather clearing, the force took off on 15 September and set course for Kaa Fjord and the *Tirpitz*. Although the vessel was clearly sighted, its smoke defences were quickly activated, effectively obscuring the battleship from view before the attack could commence. Several aircraft did not bomb at all as a result, although all the Lancasters returned safely to Yagodnik. Here, they remained for several days, before starting home. Most reached Woodhall Spa, via Lossiemouth, on the 17th, although the last one, flown by Flg Off Bob Knights, did not show up until the 21st.

Reconnaissance photographs taken on 17 September had shown that the ship was still very much afloat, and this disappointing news came shortly after the squadron was notified that Flg Off Frank Levy (in Lancaster PB416/KC-V) had flown into high ground near Nesbyn, about 100 miles north west of Oslo, with the loss of all on board. Amongst those killed were two members of Drew Wyness' crew, who had been hitching a lift home as their own aircraft was stranded in the USSR. It had been their first operation with No 617 Sqn.

After the arduous flights to and from the USSR, as well as the attack on *Tirpitz* itself, the aircrews were granted a few days' leave. This gave the hard-pressed groundcrews time to prepare the aircraft for the next operation, against the Dortmund-Ems Canal on 23 September – the scene of No 617 Sqn's terrible losses almost a year earlier. However, on this occasion the unit's aircraft would be carrying a more suitable weapon and a better bombsight.

As the Lancasters left Woodhall Spa in the early evening of the 23rd, the operation could not have been more different to the one carried out the previous year. Although thick cloud hampered crews over the target (leaving some to return with their *Tallboys*), the overall bombing was very good, with at least two direct hits made on the banks of the canal.

A reconnaissance photograph of the Dortmund-Ems Canal after the 23 September 1944 attack, showing breaches in the banks of both branches and numerous near misses, including several in the water (*Beck Parsons*)

Flt Lt Jack Sayers and his crew in late September 1943, having just been allocated DV402/KC-X. Mick Martin, who added the winged Kangaroo nose art, had previously flown this aircraft prior to it being taken over by fellow Australian, Flg Off Arthur Kell. Sayers flew DV402 on its next operation (which was its 39th) to the Westkappel Sea Wall on 3 October 1944. The bomber survived the war and was struck off charge in late November 1945 *(Colin Burgess)*

These breached both branches, while more than 100 aircraft of the main force caused further damage.

On the way home Flt Lt Geoff Stout's NF923/KC-M was attacked by a nightfighter, which succeeded in knocking out three engines. Hampered by the heavy *Tallboy* still aboard, Stout kept the aircraft flying to enable the rest of his crew to bail out, but he was killed when the Lancaster crashed seconds later. Of the others, two subsequently died of their injuries and two more were captured, spending the rest of the war as PoWs. The remaining two successfully evaded capture and succeeded in returning to the UK.

On 3 October 1944, Tait flew the Mosquito once again when his unit was tasked with breaching the sea wall at Westkapelle. However, as he arrived over the target, he could see that it had already been severely damaged by the preceding main force, so he aborted the operation and ordered the crews to return to Woodhall Spa.

KEMBS BARRAGE

With Allied troops now advancing rapidly across France towards Germany, it was feared that the enemy might try and flood the Rhine Valley in an attempt to hinder their progress. A critical point was the barrage near Kembs – a dam-like structure which lay on the Rhine just north of Basle, on the border between France, Germany and Switzerland. If the sluice gates were opened, the effect on any ground forces would be catastrophic, and so the Americans wanted it destroyed as quickly as possible to allow the waters to dissipate naturally along the river's length. So, four days after their return from Westkapelle, No 617 Sqn was detailed to bomb it, although the unit's method of attack would leave crews open to extreme danger.

The barrage over the Rhine near Kembs, which was attacked successfully by No 617 Sqn on 7 October 1944. The unit scored two near-direct hits, which destroyed the lock gates. The land to the left is France, while that to the right is Germany. Switzerland lies to the lower left of the camerama *(Bob Knights)*

The force was split into two groups, with the first (of seven) dropping their *Tallboys* from around 8000 ft, while the rest (six crews) would fly in at the same time to drop their bombs, fitted with delayed-action fuses, from just 600 ft. Although five of the Lancaster crews carried an extra gunner, a Mustang escort would be provided to give some cover from the intense flak barrage that was expected over the target.

The sky was clear as the aircraft arrived over the barrage. Tait dropped his *Tallboy* from 600 ft, and it landed close to the lock gates, while Cockshott also scored an almost direct hit. Several others obtained near misses, and the attack was deemed to be successful, putting the gates out of action. Two crew were lost, however.

Sqn Ldr Drew Wyness, who had already seen two of his original crew killed when they crashed returning from the USSR two weeks earlier, came under heavy fire, which put two of his engines out of action. He dropped his *Tallboy* and turned north, but was soon forced to ditch his Lancaster (NG180/KC-S) in the Rhine close to the town of Chalampe. What happened next is unclear, but it seems that all seven crew survived the ditching, only to possibly be executed by firing squad later that same day.

Following Wyness at low-level was Flt Lt 'Kit' Howard in Lancaster LM482/KC-Q. He had already made one unsuccessful run on the target, and was turning for a second when his bomber was hit in the starboard wing, which caught fire before disintegrating. The Lancaster crashed into a wood at Efringen-Kirchen, some two miles north of the target. Howard's crew was one of those carrying an extra gunner – Flg Off David Watkins from Flt Lt David Oram's crew – and no one survived.

BACK TO THE *TIRPITZ*

Although it remained afloat and seemingly unscathed after the September operation, *Tirpitz* had indeed been hit and damaged. However, the Kriegsmarine had decided that full repairs would be impractical, so it instead moved the ship to Tromsø, in northern Norway, to act as a floating artillery battery. The Allies were unaware of *Tirpitz's* diminished operational state, however, the vessel still being rated as a very real threat. A follow-up strike was hastily planned, therefore, being given the codename Operation *Obviate*. Again, No 617 Sqn would be accompanied by No 9 Sqn.

The move to Tromsø had now put *Tirpitz* just within range of the RAF, and in order to extend the 'legs' of the Lancaster, each aircraft was fitted with extra fuel tanks inside the fuselage and more powerful Merlin 24 engines.

The weather improved slightly as October drew to a close, and on the 28th a total of 20 Lancasters (including Flt Lt Brian Dobson's

Flg Off Carr and Flt Sgts Fisher and Flynn, Canadian bomb aimers from No 9 Sqn, pose with a number of *Tallboy* casings in the bomb dump at RAF Bardney. No 9 Sqn accompanied No 617 Sqn on all three attacks on the *Tirpitz* (*Canadian Forces Photograph*)

aircraft as a reserve) flew to RAF Lossiemouth, accompanied by 18 bombers from No 9 Sqn. Once again the aircraft refuelled here, and they were also joined by camera-equipped Lancaster PD337/JO-V from No 463 Sqn, whose job it was to film the attack. This time, however, the outward flight would take crews over the North Sea, across Norway and over Sweden, where they would rendezvous, before making the run in on the target. The return flight would last for several hours straight back across the North Sea.

On the morning of the 29th the Lancasters began to take off, approaching *Tirpitz* as dawn was breaking. Several crews hastily bombed through cloud, and smoke from the ships' own defences quickly began to obscure the target once again. Despite this, several bomb aimers reported seeing a near miss on the starboard bow, followed by an explosion and thick brown smoke pouring from the same area.

As the attack progressed and the cloud and smoke grew, several crews found it almost impossible to see anything. Indeed, Flg Off Doug Carey in NF920/KC-E *Easy Elsie* made five runs across the target before turning to make a sixth. As he approached, the bomber was hit by light flak, putting the port inner engine out of action and fracturing fuel lines. Carey quickly realised there was no hope of flying the 800 miles across open sea to Lossiemouth, so he headed for neutral Sweden instead, despite the protests of Flg Off Gerry Witherick, who complained that he had a reputation for always getting back to base! After circling the town of Porjus, Carey eventually made a crash landing in boggy ground, although he badly injured his knee as the aircraft came to rest. All six on board survived and were interned, being repatriated to the UK several months later.

Although reconnaissance photographs following this mission showed that minor damage had been inflicted on the battleship, *Tirpitz* still remained very much afloat. A third attack, codenamed Operation *Catechism*, was immediately organised. Nineteen aircraft flew to Lossiemouth on 4 November, only to be met by foul weather and near gale force winds. Unsurprisingly, the operation was cancelled, and No 617 Sqn returned to Woodhall Spa the following day. Over the next week Lincolnshire was dogged by frost, rain and high winds, making operations impossible, but as this began to break on the 11th, 19 Lancasters (plus Flt Lt Howard Gavin's aircraft as a spare) again returned

A remarkable sea-level photograph of the *Tirpitz* under attack off Håkøya Island, near Tromsø, on 12 November 1944. *Tallboy* bursts can be seen in the water, while the ship is off to the right, having just fired a salvo from her forward turret (*Bob Knights*)

The upturned hull of the *Tirpitz* following the successful attack on 12 November 1944. Of the 1700 men aboard at the time of the attack, almost 1000 were drowned, many not able to escape as it capsized so quickly. A number of holes can be seen cut into the hull, and through these 87 men were saved from compartments that they had climbed into (*Beck Parsons*)

to Lossiemouth, where they refuelled, before setting out for Norway in the early hours of 12 November.

The weather was bright and clear as the force turned and began running in over the Swedish border. When Lancasters approached the target area at just before 0830 hrs, *Tirpitz* could be easily seen. German fighters were scrambled, but they were directed to the wrong place, leaving the ship at the mercy of the RAF. Even though the smoke defences on board were again quickly deployed, they proved unable to save the vessel on this occasion. Lancaster crews reported several direct hits, as well as a number of near misses, and as the last bombs fell the leviathan lurched in the water and capsized. The *Tirpitz* threat was finally over.

Although several crews landed at Lossiemouth because of low fuel, the rest flew directly back to Woodhall Spa, where they were greeted by jubilant groundcrews. The band of the Border Regiment had also been hastily assembled, and it played the RAF March Past and other rousing tunes as the aircraft taxied in.

The scene over the next few days was reminiscent of the period after the Dams raid in May 1943, with crews posing for official photographs next to their aircraft, and messages of congratulations pouring in from all quarters. Tait himself flew down to London for a radio broadcast about the attack, and was interviewed by the press, who quickly coined the nickname '*Tirpitz* Tait'. He returned to Woodhall Spa on 15 November (the day after the remaining crews had flown in from Lossiemouth) for a lunch with the Secretary of State for Air Sir Archibald Sinclair, before flying back to London again later that same day for another press conference. His crews meanwhile, were given a very welcome 48 hours' leave.

As December began, so the weather closed in, curtailing both training flights and operations. Three of the latter were scheduled and then cancelled in the first week alone, including an operation to the Urft Dam on the 7th, which was postponed until the following day. This was to be

The day after the successful sinking of the *Tirpitz*, a series of photographs were taken of the crews by their aircraft. Wg Cdr '*Tirpitz* Tait' (fifth from left), as the press nicknamed him, is seen with his own aircraft, EE146/KC-D, although unaccountably the crew is that of Flg Off Ross Stanford's (standing third from left), who did not actually fly on any of the three attacks on the ship! (*IWM Neg No CH17864*)

a repeat of the Kembs Barrage almost two months previously, but on this occasion the 19 crews found a thick blanket of cloud covering the target, and so were ordered back to base. Although no flak was reported over the target, two crews were hit by a gun situated to the north as they circled the area, while Sqn Ldr John Brookes (in DV385/KC-V) was hit as he returned over Dunkirk. His navigator, Flg Off Jack Jones, recalled that they had descended to a few hundred feet for a 'stooge around', whereupon everything seemed to open up at them.

No 617 Sqn tried again on 11 December, this time with better conditions, but despite several near misses and at least one direct hit, the bombers left the target and surrounding banks largely undamaged.

The unit returned to Ijmuiden again on 15 December to attack the E-boat pens in a similar operation to the one mounted back in August, and despite a smokescreen, results were good and several pens received direct hits. But the flak was also accurate, and a number of aircraft were damaged, including PB415/KC-O flown by Sqn Ldr 'Jock' Calder. It was hit in the centre section, shearing the main spar on the starboard side outboard of the No.4 engine. Amazingly, the aircraft held together, and Calder turned for home, gradually losing height across

A reconnaissance photograph of the E- and R-Boat pens at Ijmuiden, in Holland, after the daylight raid on 15 December 1944. The pens are ringed by numerous *Tallboy* craters, while the roof of the west pen (lower in the photograph) has partially collapsed after two bombs pierced the reinforced concrete and exploded inside (*IWM Neg No C4885*)

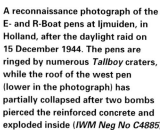

the sea whilst he battled with the controls. Heavy vibrations continually shook the aircraft, but he arrived over the emergency airfield at Woodbridge, in Suffolk, where he made a successful landing.

Ijmuiden was notable for another reason as well, for it proved to be Tait's last mission with No 617 Sqn. After 101 operations he was to be grounded. The bad weather in December continued to dog the unit, with operations scheduled for the 18th and 19th both being cancelled. Conditions were not much better on the 21st when the squadron flew to Politz, on the north German coast, to attack the oil refinery there. Aside from

After relinquishing his rank of air commodore so that he could return to operational flying, Canadian Grp Capt Johnnie Fauquier took over from Tait as No 617 Sqn's new CO in December 1944. Not everyone liked the more aggressive style he brought to the unit. Fauquier retired from the RCAF in 1946 (*Canadian Forces Photograph*)

the fact that it was to be a long trip (lasting around ten hours), and No 617 Sqn's first night operation for several months, for once the target marking was not to be done in-house.

Sixteen Lancasters, led by Sqn Ldr Johnny Cockshott, formed part of a main force of more than 200 aircraft that found the target obscured by cloud and smoke. Although the bombing was scattered over a wide area, the plant was damaged in several places. However, the weather had not finished with them for the night, and as the crews returned, heavy fog meant a diversion to RAF Ludford Magna, which was equipped with FIDO (Fog, Intensive, Dispersal Operation – a set of pipes filled with petrol that ran the length of the runway on each side which, when lit, literally burnt off the fog) equipment.

As he was circling the area preparing to land, Flg Off Arthur Joplin (in ME561/KC-T) briefly struck the ground, sending a violent shudder through the aircraft. As he battled to keep control, he ordered the rest of the crew to assume crash positions moments before coming down near Market Rasen at 0240 hrs. The bomber slid to a halt a few hundred yards further on. Regaining their senses, the crew staggered from the wreckage, but they were only five in number. Bomb aimer Flg Off Arthur Walker and mid-upper gunner Flg Off Roberton Yates were both dead.

The onset of more poor weather saw No 617 Sqn initially grounded as Christmas arrived, and then finally stood down on the morning of the 25th. Three days later the unit threw a party for its outgoing commanding officer, who was now to use his expertise to help train Canadian bomber crews. Tait had been flying on operations almost constantly for five years, completing four tours.

When he assumed command of No 617 Sqn, Tait held two DSOs, a DFC and two MiDs. Tait gained a third DSO in September 1944 and a second DFC three months later. Having come to the end to his operational flying, he was initially recommended for a VC for 'sustained gallantry', but unlike his predecessor Leonard Cheshire, Tait eventually received a fourth DSO – unprecedented in the RAF.

FAUQUIER TAKES OVER

The calibre of aircrew serving with No 617 Sqn had always been high, but the men chosen to lead the unit were amongst the best commanders and pilots Bomber Command could offer. Tait's successor, Canadian Grp Capt John Fauquier, continued this tradition.

Flying as a bush pilot before joining the RCAF in 1939, Fauquier had served as an instructor in the British Commonwealth Air Training Plan (BCATP) prior to being posted to the UK, where he joined, and then commanded, No 405 Sqn (punctuated by a short spell as a Staff Officer). Completing a second tour of operations in January 1944, he was promoted to air commodore and moved to a job at HQ No 6 Group (RCAF), where he served as Senior Operations Staff Officer. At the time Fauquier's rank precluded him from operational flying, but upon hearing that AVM Cochrane was looking for a successor to Tait, he immediately offered to relinquish his rank and applied, eventually being offered the job.

Although No 617 Sqn had from the outset contained crews from across the Empire, Fauquier was its first non-British commanding officer.

After his Lancaster (NF992/KC-B) was attacked by fighters over Bergen on the 12 January 1944 raid, Flg Off Ian Ross was seen to ditch in the sea. No trace was later found of him or his crew, and it has been thought that they were possibly machine-gunned in the water later that same day (*Colin Burgess*)

Despite completing two operational tours and having been awarded two DSOs, a DFC and a MiD along the way, his appointment was met with unease by some who did not initially take to his aggressive style. It was obvious he would have to prove himself, although the squadron had more pressing matters for now – an operation to bomb the E-boat pens at Rotterdam, in Holland, was scheduled for 29 December.

Sixteen aircraft, led by 'Jock' Calder, took off just after lunch and easily found the target in the clear afternoon sky. Several direct hits were made, although crews were not so lucky the following day when they embarked on a similar operation to Ijmuiden once again. With low cloud covering the target, and more moving in, Calder, who was again leading, decided to abort the operation.

Fauquier got his first opportunity to lead No 617 Sqn on the last night of 1944 when the unit was detailed for an operation to Oslo to find and attack the German cruisers *Köln* and *Emden*. Taking off just before 2000 hrs, both vessels were found moving at full speed outside the harbour, but despite a number of near misses they escaped unscathed. It was later discovered, however, that in attempting to outrun the falling bombs, one of the warships had run aground on a sandbank. By the time No 617 Sqn returned to Woodhall Spa, 1945 had arrived.

January began as December had ended, with biting cold winds seeing the familiar routine of operations being scheduled then cancelled. This continued into the second week of 1945, but when conditions began to clear on the 10th, an operation to Bergen harbour, in Norway, was scheduled for 48 hours later. Accompanied by aircraft from No 9 Sqn once again, three No 617 Sqn Lancasters were briefed to attack shipping in the harbour, while the rest targeted boat pens and a floating dock. The former received three direct hits, but as he circled the harbour (in Mosquito NT205/L), Fauquier noticed that the smoke from the attack was beginning to obscure the target. He therefore ordered those aircraft that had yet to bomb to aim for the ships, several of which were successfully hit and sunk.

Although Flt Lt John Pryor had already made several runs over the target, he had been frustrated each time, so he turned in for another attempt. As he did so his aircraft (PD233/KC-G) came under attack from a pair of Fw 190 fighters that succeeded in putting two of the Lancaster's engines out of action. With the bomber badly damaged and difficult to control, Pryor gave the order to bail out. WO Ernie Temple, who had survived the crash of Lancaster ED765/AJ-M in August 1943, did so again, spending the rest of the war as a PoW. Bomb aimer Flg Off George Kendrick was not so lucky, being found later with severe scalp and back injuries after his parachute had failed to deploy. Rushed to hospital, he died from his injuries three days later.

Kendrick's death was particularly poignant, for he had survived a crash during training in January 1944 when flying in 'Dambuster' Lancaster ED918/AJ-F. Having fought for almost a year to regain full health, he had only rejoined No 617 Sqn a few weeks before his death.

Following Pryor in over the target was Flg Off Ian Ross in NF992/KC-B, and his aircraft was also hit by fighters. With his starboard inner engine knocked out and the flight controls damaged, Ross ordered the crew to jettison the *Tallboy*, prior to successfully ditching in the sea. Several other Lancaster crews witnessed the survivors scrambling out of the fuselage to stand on the wings, and soon an ASR aircraft was seen overhead. It dropped a lifeboat, but nothing more was heard from the downed crew. Despite an extensive search through the night, no trace was found of the crew or the lifeboat. This led to speculation in No 617 Sqn that Ross and his men may have been strafed by one of the German fighters later that same day. In March, the body of wireless operator Flg Off Mowbray Ellwood was washed ashore. He had left a young wife in England.

The fighters almost claimed a third victim when they singled out Sqn Ldr Tony Iveson's NG181/KC-M as the bomber made its run. With a severely damaged tail and rear turret, and with the port inner engine on fire, Iveson immediately told the crew to prepare to bail out as he continued grappling with the controls. Eventually, the fighters gave up the attack, and he gently turned for home, landing at Woodhall Spa some time later after also being engaged by flak. Once back at base, it was quickly realised that the wireless operator and mid-upper and rear gunners were not on board. They had bailed out after misinterpreting the order, but survived to be taken prisoner.

Following the Bergen raid the weather clamped in again, preventing operations. At the same time Fauquier received an instruction to supply six crews to fly down to the south coast to participate in trials of a new weapon known as a 'Boom Patrol Boat', which was being developed by the Operations Division of the Admiralty. It consisted of a small launch-type craft whose bow was filled with explosive. After being carried to the target by an aircraft, the boat would be dropped into the sea, complete with a two-man crew, under three large parachutes. After a successful touchdown, the canopies would be discarded, the engines switched on and the boat piloted towards its target.

Four Lancasters were lightly modified at Woodhall Spa with carriers and other ancillary equipment to allow a boat to be carried, with a crew, on the trials, which were codenamed Exercise *Teignmouth II*. The original plan called for four aircraft to take part on the first day, after which two Lancasters would land at Exeter aerodrome to have the additional equipment removed, while the other two would fly back to Woodhall Spa, so that the remaining two crews could use them to complete the trials the following day.

A poor but rare photograph showing a 'Boom Patrol Boat' just after release from Lancaster DV393/KC-), flown by Flg Off Phil Martin, during Operation *Teignmouth II* on 17 January 1945. The boat, complete with its 'crew' of one Royal Marine volunteer and a kitbag, dropped to an almost vertical attitude, before righting itself under three parachutes

95

The 'Boom Patrol Boat' descends under its three canopies before alighting on the sea, after which the canopies detached automatically. Four Lancasters participated in the exercise, which was seemingly a success

During the morning of 17 January, the initial four crews prepared for the exercise. Incredibly, each would be carrying 'live' cargo in the form of a single Royal Marine volunteer in each boat, plus a weighted kitbag. As there was no way for the volunteer Marine to board the boat in flight, he embarked during the loading phase at Woodhall Spa before take-off, being in contact with the Lancaster crew throughout the flight via the intercom. Due to the size and depth of the boat, the take-off and flight to the exercise area was made with the bomb-bay doors open and the vessel protruding underneath.

The crews left Woodhall Spa and flew in formation down to the test area at Teignmouth, near Exeter, on the south coast, arriving just after midday. The test area was clearly visible as they approached, being marked out on the sea as a large yellow rectangle with a smoke candle burning in the centre to monitor the wind direction. After making contact with the controller for the exercise (a Royal Marines captain who was on board an RAF ASR launch), they orbited the area awaiting further instructions.

Having been given permission to proceed, Flg Off Phil Martin lined up DV393/KC-R and flew across the test area to ascertain the wind direction for the first drop, before circling round and releasing his boat from 2000 ft whilst flying at 140 mph. It fell at an alarming, near vertical, angle before righting itself as the parachutes deployed, descending gracefully until gently touching down on the sea. After a short pause, the other crews (Sqn Ldrs Tony Iveson and Charles Hamilton and Flg Off Freddy Watts) repeated the exercise, although they dropped their boats from 1000 ft.

In the event, all the drops went surprisingly well, despite the parachutes snagging and ripping as they left the aircraft on all but Hamilton's drop. Although the fearless Royal Marines who were aboard the boats as they fell were reported to be 'enthusiastic and satisfied that the exercise was a success', Flg Off Martin commented 'that bloody Marine officer treated those brave commandos like shit!' – a sentiment shared by Flt Sgt Don Day, his bomb aimer.

With the trials complete, Hamilton and Iveson flew straight back to Woodhall, while Martin and Watts (who was flying DV405/KC-J) landed at Exeter to allow the additional equipment to be removed, after which they too returned to base. In the event, the two remaining crews who were due to complete the exercise the following day (Flt Lt Howard Gavin and Flg Off James Castagnola) were not needed.

There was, naturally, a great deal of speculation as to how the boats and No 617 Sqn would be used. Although the crews were ordered not to discuss the nature of the stores they had dropped, rumours surfaced about possible attacks on U-boat pens, and also difficult-to-reach targets such as the heavy water plants in Norway, which were being used by the Germans for research into nuclear weapons. Ultimately, the boats were never used in anger, and there is nothing in surviving official reports to suggest that No 617 Sqn's part in their potential use was to be anything more than assistance in the trials. One of the more bizarre chapters in No 617 Sqn's wartime history was over in just 24 hours.

Although most of the remaining 'Dambuster' Lancasters had been sent to RAF Metheringham for storage in mid-1944, six had remained with No 617 Sqn at Woodhall Spa (ED817, ED909, ED912, ED915, ED921 and ED929). By the end of the year it had finally been decided that there was no immediate prospect that they, or *Upkeep*, would be used again. Accordingly, with the agreement of ACM Harris, No 5 Group ordered the squadron to send all of the aircraft to No 41 Group at RAF Lossiemouth for storage, where they were to be kept at seven days' readiness. Aside from the six modified aircraft at Woodhall Spa, there were also several others at RAF Coningsby, where they had been used in various trials and other work. All were duly ferried to Lossiemouth over the last few days of January and into the first week of February.

On 3 February, No 617 Sqn was detailed for only its second operation since New Year, to Pootershaven, in Holland. Eighteen aircraft, led by Fauquier in NG445/KC-E, bombed the midget submarine pens, while 18 Lancasters from No 9 Sqn headed for Ijmuiden with a similar mission tasking. A short operation (lasting around three-and-a-half hours for most crews), it was a great success, with No 617 Sqn scoring several direct hits and destroying almost all of the facility.

Three days later the unit flew to Germany to attack the Bielefeld Viaduct – a vitally important target carrying an important rail link – but the 17 aircraft sent on the operation found the area covered in ten-tenths cloud and returned without bombing.

Following a trip to Ijmuiden on the 8th to attack the E-boat pens once again (when accurate bombing collapsed much of the roof, blocking the pens with hundreds of tons of rubble, which finally put them out of action), No 617 Sqn returned again to Bielefeld on Valentine's Day. This second attempt encountered similar conditions to the first, with thick cloud obscuring the target, so again the operation was aborted. A third attempt was made on the 22nd, but even with a clear view of the target and several near misses, only slight damage was inflicted, which the Germans quickly repaired. One last operation was detailed before the end of the month against an undamaged stretch of the Dortmund-Ems Canal, but again the target was obscured by thick cloud and the mission was aborted. This was a rather dismal end to a frustrating month.

GRANDSLAM

Although the six-tonne *Tallboy* bomb had been proven in action on numerous occasions, the original concept of Barnes Wallis had been for a weapon weighing ten tonnes. With ever increasing improvements to the Lancaster, Wallis' dream of the ten-tonne version could now become a reality. This larger weapon, christened *Grandslam*, was identical in shape and construction to *Tallboy*, but was 10,000 lbs heavier and 4 ft 5 in longer. It too featured four offset fins on the tail to revolve the bomb as it fell (reaching a maximum rotational velocity of 60 rpm), and was suspended in the bomb-bay by the same linked 'chain' as used on *Tallboy*, only extended to accommodate *Grandslam*'s considerably greater girth.

A batch of 32 Lancasters was completed specifically to carry *Grandslam*, these aircraft being given the designation B I (Special). Reminiscent of the original 'Dambusting' machines, each one had its bomb-bay doors removed and the bay fitted with aerodynamic fairings at each end. More powerful Rolls-Royce Merlin 24 engines and a stronger undercarriage would help bear the huge weight of the 22,000-lb weapon.

The first two modified airframes (PB592 and PB995) were sent to Boscombe Down to undertake flight trials both with and without the weapon aboard, while the next few were delivered straight to Woodhall Spa. The Boscombe trials resulted in a recommendation that the front turret be removed and faired over in order to save weight. The deletion of internal equipment such as the Elsan lavatory, radios and the navigator's chair (the latter replaced with a wicker one) also helped lighten the Lancaster, and thus help increase its range. After the bombers' arrival, groundcrews made additional modifications, which in some cases saw the removal of the mid-upper turret as well. Finally, the new squadron code 'YZ' were allocated only to these modified aircraft.

Fauquier flew one (PB997/YZ-E) for the first time on 5 March, and found it to be both fast and responsive.

An unidentified Lancaster B I (Special) in the night camouflage scheme that was first used on these aircraft. Armed with a 22,000-lb *Grandslam* it is having its engines run up out at dispersal in March 1945 (*Beck Parsons*)

With the removal of two turrets, the bomb-bay doors and many internal items, the B I (Special) Lancasters flew like fighters when not carrying a bomb load. With no need to mute the glowing exhausts during the daylight operations, the shrouds were also removed from each engine cowling (*Colin Burgess*)

As the Bielefeld Viaduct was deemed to be a top priority target, a fourth attempt was made on 9 March, but incredibly the unit's efforts were thwarted yet again by the weather, and the crews ordered to return to base. However, it presented the ideal opportunity to try *Grandslam* operationally, so another attack was planned using several of the new weapons to supplement a *Tallboy* attack.

Incredibly, no live trial had yet taken place with the weapon, the first being scheduled for the morning of 13 March – the same day as the raid! The result of the trial was eagerly awaited, therefore, and it proved to be a complete success. Dropped over the Ashley Walk bombing range, the bomb left a crater some 130 ft wide and more than 30 ft deep. With this successful drop behind it, *Grandslam* was now cleared for use.

Two hours later 20 aircraft took off from Woodhall Spa, bound for the Bielefeld Viaduct. Included in the formation's ranks were

USAAF pilot Lt Bill Adams (fourth from left) is seen here with his crew in front of newly delivered B I (Special) PD113 in early March 1945, although he never actually flew the aircraft operationally. Like most of the initial B I (Special) Lancasters, PD113 was delivered to No 617 Sqn with both mid-upper and rear turrets (as can be seen by the fairing for the mid-upper turret on top of the fuselage), which it retained for its first operation to the Arnsberg Viaduct on 19 March 1945, carrying a six-man crew, and coded YZ-T. The mid-upper turret was removed for subsequent operations, however (*Tom Collins*)

A low-level view of the Bielefeld Viaduct after the attack on 14 March 1945. This was the first occasion *Grandslam* was used operationally, and a single bomb was enough to bring down eight arches, while several *Tallboys* caused further damage to the structure and railway lines

Having joined No 617 Sqn in late August 1944, Flg Off Phil Martin was immediately thrown into the fray, his first operation being against the *Tirpitz* in mid-September. On 19 March 1945, he dropped a *Grandslam* on the Arnsburg Viaduct, the weapon overshooting by a mere 30 yards. Strangely, although Martin's Lancaster had the mid-upper turret removed, the squadron records state that both gunners were on board (but no wireless operator), while the pilot's own log records that he carried all six of his crew! (*Phil Martin*)

Fauquier and 'Jock' Calder (in PD119/YZ-J and PD112/YZ-S, respectively), carrying the only two live *Grandslams* then in existence. As both the front and mid-upper turrets had been faired over, only the rear gunner remained, whilst the omission of the radio sets meant that the wireless operator also stayed behind, leaving a five-man crew. Unbelievably, thick cloud came to the rescue of the viaduct yet again, and the crews turned for home without bombing.

In the case of Fauquier and Calder, with the increased weight of the *Grandslam* adversely affecting the bombers' roll out on landing, both pilots diverted to RAF Carnaby, as it had a longer runway than Woodhall Spa. No 5 Group was eager to put the target out of action once and for all, however, so it hastily scheduled a return visit for the following day.

In an effort to reduce strain placed on the airframe and undercarriage by the *Grandslam* bomb, both weapons were removed by groundcrews bussed over to Carnaby from Woodhall Spa. They continued to work on the two Lancasters in preparation for the mission the following day, and by 1300 hrs on the 14th, all was ready. However, as the two pilots went through their checks and prepared to start engines, Fauquier found he had a problem with his starboard inner Merlin. A broken connecting rod meant that his Lancaster would be going nowhere, leaving Calder's crew to potentially make history by being the first to drop the largest bomb in the world.

Refusing to give up on the mission, Fauquier clambered out of his Lancaster and raced over to Calder's machine in the vain hope of commandeering the aircraft. However, the Scot saw his commander sprinting across the tarmac and realised what must have happened. Mischievously turning a 'blind eye', Calder opened the throttles and roared down the runway, taking off at 1348 hrs. Stuck firmly on the ground, Fauquier watched as the Lancaster disappeared from view.

The force consisted of 32 Lancasters from Nos 9 (detailed to attack the Arnsberg Viaduct) and 617 Sqns, accompanied by four *Oboe*-equipped Mosquitos from No 8 Group. Although there was patchy cloud over the target, conditions were far better than they had been 24 hours earlier, and

A still from the film showing Martin's B I (Special) PB996/YZ-C still in its night camouflage scheme, after he had dropped his *Grandslam* on the Arnsberg Viaduct on 19 March 1945. The 'arms' hanging underneath are the suspension 'chain' used to hold the bomb, having been pulled back up by a member of the crew. The light area on top of the fuselage is where the mid-upper turret had been removed (*IWM Neg No CH15376*)

Calder was determined not to have any reason to abort his drop. After a short run, he released his *Grandslam* from just under 12,000 ft, while the Lancaster, relieved of its ten-tonne payload, immediately shot upwards for about 500 ft. Calder regained his composure, and control, and brought the bomber round to view the result.

Although the weapon undershot the target by about 30 yards, the immense shock wave from the explosion brought down almost 260 ft of viaduct, while several direct or near-direct *Tallboy* hits had further damaged the structure and nearby rail lines. The No 617 Sqn crews returned to Woodhall Spa in a jubilant mood to be met by their commander, who although happy at the result, was furious at Calder. Although he never really forgave him, Fauquier did recommend Calder for a second DSO, which was duly gazetted in June 1945.

No 617 Sqn had succeeded in destroying the Bielefeld Viaduct, but No 9 Sqn had fared less well at the Arnsburg, so the following day (15 March) the unit returned for another try, accompanied by Calder and Sqn Ldr

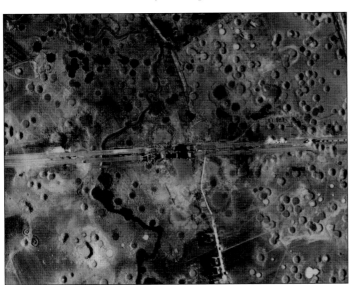

A vertical reconnaissance photograph of the Bielefeld Viaduct on 15 March 1945, showing the destroyed central section, as well as dozens of other craters from previous attempts to bomb the target

In this posed photograph, taken on 24 March 1945, a *Grandslam* – the largest conventional bomb of the war – is seen about to be loaded onto its special trolley in the bomb dump at Woodhall Spa. The wooden packing crates for the lightweight aluminium tail section can be seen behind the weapons (*Canadian Forces Photograph*)

Cockshot, carrying a *Grandslam* each. The target was enveloped by cloud once again, and only Cockshott dropped his bomb. Even with the rest using *Tallboys*, the viaduct was left relatively undamaged, so on the 19th No 617 Sqn tried alone, this time using six *Grandslams* and thirteen *Tallboys*. With clear weather allowing for accurate aiming, the viaduct did not stand a chance. A 40-ft section was destroyed, putting it out of action for the rest of the war.

No 617 Sqn was next detailed to attack the Arbergen rail bridge near Bremen on 21 March. Twenty aircraft, including Fauquier and Calder with *Grandslams*, bombed accurately, destroying the target, but not before Flt Lt Bernard Gumbley (in PD117/YZ-L) was hit by flak in the tail. His Lancaster immediately turned over and dived into the ground in flames near Okel, killing all five crewmen.

Although *Grandslam* and *Tallboy* were proving highly effective, there was some concern at No 5 Group at the rate at which they were being used. Expensive and difficult to produce, few of the bombs were completed in the same time that it took to build conventional ordnance, and use was outstripping supply. On 16 March Fauquier had attended a conference to discuss this problem, and delegates came up with the following solution.

Upon reaching the target, four aircraft would bomb and their results observed *before* the next four (if needed) would follow up, and so on. The plan was agreed, and it would be tried on the unit's very next operation, against the Neinburg rail bridge, near Hanover, on 22 March.

An armament officer checks complete *Grandslams* in the bomb dump at Woodhall Spa before they are loaded onto trolleys and taken out to the waiting aircraft. One (at top) has yet to have its tail section fitted (*Beck Parsons*)

It is interesting to note that from the extremely hazardous days of night operations some 18 months before, No 617 Sqn was now at liberty to monitor bombing effects during an operation thanks to the virtual non-existence of German fighters and flak.

Of the 20 aircraft that took off for Neinburg, 14 carried *Tallboys* and the remaining six *Grandslams*. After the first four had bombed, Fauquier dived down to observe the results, before ordering the next four in. The technique was very successful, and the bridge was destroyed with two *Tallboys* and a *Grandslam* remaining. The following day an identical force bombed another rail bridge near Bremen with equal success, although they were harassed over the target by Me 262 jet fighters and heavy flak. The latter damaged several aircraft, including Flt Lt Lancey's NG489/KC-M, which had its bombsight put out of action.

On 27 March a combined force of 115 aircraft from No 5 Group flew to Farge, just north of Bremen, with 95 bombers detailed to attack an oil storage depot and the other 20 (all from No 617 Sqn) the almost complete U-boat pens. The latter were huge concrete structures (the largest in the world at the time) some 1450 ft long, 300 ft wide and more than 75 ft high, with roofs made of reinforced concrete 23 ft thick. Some measure of how important the target was considered to be can be gauged by the fact that 14 *Grandslams* were taken in the hope that the pens would be neutralised in a single operation.

NIENBURG R.R.BRIDGE
K-4071 (Immen)
Dist 23C

The Weser Bridge at Nienberg, which was bombed with *Grandslam* and *Tallboy* on 22 March 1945. For the first time, only a handful of bombs were dropped, with the results observed before the next few were released. Five large *Grandslam* craters can be seen (one in the water) very close to the bridge, while numerous *Tallboy* ones litter the surrounding area

Flt Lt Jack Sayers and his crew with PD113/YZ-T, which they took to Farge on 27 March 1945. When B I (Special) Lancasters operated, they generally only carried a crew of five, as they lacked radio sets and front and upper turrets. Seen here, from left to right, are Plt Off Weaver (bomb aimer), Flg Off Barry (rear gunner), Flt Lt Sayers (pilot) and Flg Offs Johnson (flight engineer) and Wittmer (navigator) (*Colin Burgess*)

Six Canadian members of the squadron paste a 'Victory Loans' poster to the nose of a *Tallboy* at Woodhall Spa on 2 April 1945. Sitting on the bomb, from left to right, are Flt Lts Lancey (pilot) and Price (pilot), Flg Off Kelly (bomb aimer to Flt Lt Hill) and Flt Lts English (rear gunner to Flt Lt Lancey) and Hill (pilot). 'Pasting' the poster at front is Lancey's mid-upper gunner, Flg Off Jennison (*Canadian Forces Photograph*)

An RAF officer inspects the hole left by a *Grandslam* in the reinforced concrete roof of the submarine pens at Farge, in Germany, after the daylight raid by No 617 Sqn on 27 March 1945. Two direct *Grandslam* hits caused most of the roof to collapse (*IWM Neg No CL2607*)

Although two crews returned with minor engine problems, the rest reached the target without incident and began their bombing runs just after 1300 hrs. Flak hampered most of them, with a number of aircraft being hit. However, Flg Off Bill Richardson, navigator to Flt Lt Trent, thought that the jolt the *Grandslam* gave the Lancaster as it left the aircraft was far bigger than any near flak hit he had ever encountered. The results were spectacular, with two *Grandslams* penetrating the roofs and bringing down thousands of tons of rubble and masonry. There would be no need for a return visit.

THE FINAL STRETCH

With the German war machine now in total disarray, the end of the European war was in sight. There was no let-up for the No 617 Sqn crews, however, who spent most of the first week of April flying intensive training exercises, both by day and by night. Their first

operation of the month was on the 6th, when 14 aircraft flew to Ijmuiden again to bomb shipping, although ten-tenths cloud over the target left Calder (leading in place of Fauquier, who was away on leave) with no option but to abort the operation and return to base. With the weather improving the following day, the same force returned, this time led by Sqn Ldr Cockshott. Three direct hits and several near misses were claimed on the quay and ships in the harbour.

Although operations were detailed for the following day, these were subsequently cancelled and the squadron stood down until the following afternoon (9 April), when 17 crews flew to Hamburg to bomb U-boat pens. Spitfires and Mustangs accompanied them to provide fighter cover, although in the event no opposition was encountered over the

A *Tallboy* bomb in the bomb-bay of Lancaster B I (Special) PD129/YZ-O on 2 April 1945. Although built to carry the *Grandslam*, B I (Special) Lancasters actually carried more *Tallboys* on operations. To accommodate the smaller bomb, the suspension 'chain' was simply moved up a link, with the topmost left loose. It can be seen at the top of the 'chain', resting inwards against the body of the bomb (*Canadian Forces Photograph*)

Bomb bursts over the U-boat pens at Hamburg on 9 April 1945. With the end of the war close, no opposition was found over the target, and the pens and docks were left severely damaged (*Colin Burgess*)

A *Grandslam*, seen on its special bomb trolley at Woodhall Spa in April 1945 from under the wing of B I (Special) PD129/YZ-O, in a posed photograph taken on 2 April 1945 (*Canadian Forces Photograph*)

target. The aiming was good and the bombing concentrated, and the pens and harbour installations were left severely damaged.

After a respite of several days, No 617 Sqn flew to Swinemünde on 13 April to bomb the German pocket battleship *Lützow* and the heavy cruiser *Prinz Eugen*. Some 14 Lancasters from No 9 Sqn were also involved, but the weather protected the Germans and the operation was abandoned. A similar force tried again two days later but met with the same result.

With two abortive attempts in two days, a third operation was scheduled for 16 April, although it was to concentrate on the *Lützow*,

Three members of the squadron pose with a *Grandslam* at Woodhall Spa on 2 April 1945 in front of BI (Special) PD129/YZ-O, which has its individual code letter also painted on the faired-over nose. The aircraft has already been bombed up with a *Tallboy*, the nose of which can just be seen in the bomb bay (*Canadian Forces Photograph*)

A number of Canadian groundcrew members of No 617 Sqn sit astride a *Grandslam* at Woodhall Spa on 2 April 1945, emphasising the weapon's enormous size. The B I (Special) behind them is PD129/YZ-O (*Canadian Forces Photograph*)

as the *Prinz Eugen* was reported to have sailed. Fauquier, though, was concerned that heavy fighter opposition would be encountered, as the Germans had had plenty of notice of the RAF's interest in the target. Fighter cover was provided, but in the event the Lancasters were not troubled over the target by the Luftwaffe. Flak, however, was intense, and few aircraft survived unscathed.

During his run in, Sqn Ldr John Powell (in NG228/KC-V) received a direct hit in the port fuel tanks, which set the aircraft on fire and probably injured some of the crew. As flames engulfed the bomber, its wing failed and broke off. The doomed Lancaster entered a dive before crashing into a wood close to the target area. Despite a parachute being reported, all seven on board died, Powell and his crew becoming the last operational casualties suffered by No 617 Sqn during World War 2. After the remaining crews returned to Woodhall Spa, the entire squadron was stood down from operations because of a lack of serviceable aircraft. This had never happened to No 617 Sqn before, and it is a clear indication of just how intense the flak barrage over Swinemünde had been.

A staged photograph, also taken on 2 April 1945, showing Grp Capt Fauquier's B I (Special) PD119/YZ-J out at dispersal with a *Grandslam* bomb, although its next operation to the U-boat pens at Hamburg was not for another week. PD119 had initially flown with an all-camouflaged tailfin, but this was changed to a half-black/half-white scheme on the outer surfaces in an attempt to help identify it as the leader's aircraft during daylight operations. The aircraft later went to No 15 Sqn for use in Operation *Front Line* at the end of the war, surviving until September 1950 when it was struck off charge and scrapped (*Canadian Forces Photograph*)

Flt Lt Hill and his bomb aimer Flg Off Kelly (centre) are debriefed by Sqn Ldr Pickard, a squadron Intelligence Officer, in April 1945 (*Canadian Forces Photograph*)

Several days would pass before operations recommenced, with 20 aircraft sent to Heligoland (a group of islands off the northwest tip of Germany) on 19 April to bomb coastal batteries and an airfield. A force of 869 aircraft had bombed the same target the previous day, and what remained was accurately targeted by Nos 617 and 9 Sqns, with the former dropping the last six *Grandslams* to be expended during the European war.

Although no operations were flown over the following week, news was received on 20 April that the *Lützow*, which No 617 Sqn had bombed four days before, had indeed been sunk. Reconnaissance photographs taken shortly after the mission appeared to reveal that the vessel had suffered little damage. However, it was later realised that the attack had ripped out the bottom of the ship's hull, leaving it to settle on the seabed in an upright position. Ever one to gain the upper hand whenever it could, the Royal Navy promptly denied that the *Lützow* had indeed been properly sunk, as it had not slipped beneath the waves!

No 617 Sqn's final operation in April came on the 25th when it conducted a token raid on Hitler's mountain retreat at Berchtesgaden and the nearby SS barracks at Obersalzburg. The unit contributed 16 Lancasters (a mixture of standard and *Grandslam* types all carrying *Tallboys*) to a combined force of 375 aircraft, including 16 Mosquitos from Nos 1, 5 and 8 Groups. Identification of the primary target proved difficult because of cloud and snow over the mountaintops, with the result that bombing was scattered. Indeed, three crews did not bomb at all, two could not see where their bombs landed and two more suffered ordnance 'hang-ups'. However, the rest caused much damage to the complex, as well as nearby bridges and junctions.

This operation proved to be the last of the war for No 617 Sqn, and it was notable for another reason too. Within Flt Lt Ian Marshall's crew were Flg Offs Len Sumpter and Ray Wilkinson, who had both flown on the unit's first operation to the Dams in May 1943.

The Berchtesgaden raid had not been led by Fauquier, who had been ordered to cease operational flying. With the war over, his work was

done, although he was still bitterly disappointed at having not been able to take part in this final mission. This was clearly evident at the pre-raid briefing when he told Sqn Ldr John Brooks, who led the raid, that he desperately wanted the operation in his logbook. As he relinquished his post, Fauquier was awarded a fourth DSO and reinstatement to his former rank of air commodore.

The man who stepped into his shoes as No 617 Sqn's last wartime commander was Wg Cdr John Evelyn Grindon, who officially took over on 28 April 1945. Following in the tradition of most of his

No 617 Sqn's last operation of the war was on 25 April 1945, when it formed part of a combined force of 375 aircraft that bombed the SS barracks at Hitler's mountain retreat of Berchtesgaden. Lancasters can be seen silhouetted against the snow-covered mountains en route to the target (*IWM Neg No CL2673*)

The crew of Flt Lt Bob Horsley pose in front of a B I (Special). They are, from left to right, Sgt Farino (rear gunner), Flt Sgt Durose (wireless operator), Flg Off Barleycorn (navigatgor), Flt Lt Bob Horsley (pilot), WO Armstrong (flight engineer) and Flt Sgts Wilson (bomb aimer) and Neale (mid-upper gunner). Horsley had originally flown as a wireless operator with No 106 Sqn, flying as part of Plt Off Leslie Manser's crew during an operation to Cologne in May 1942 when his pilot was awarded a posthumous VC. Despite being shot down, Horsley had evaded capture, making his way back to the UK, where he remustered as a pilot and duly joined No 617 Sqn from No 5 Lancaster Finishing School on 25 November 1944 (*Bob Horsley*)

No 617 Sqn's last wartime CO was Wg Cdr John Grindon, another experienced bomber pilot who was posted in on 28 April 1945 – just ten days before VE Day. As the unit had already flown its last operation of the European war by then, he instead prepared it for operations in the Far East as part of Tiger Force, which was subsequently cancelled after the dropping of the atomic bombs on Hiroshima and Nagasaki (*John Grindon*)

predecessors, Grindon was a pre-war officer educated at Cranwell, from where he had graduated in 1937. Upon the outbreak of war he went to France, flying Fairey Battles with No 150 Sqn as part of the Allied Expeditionary Force, before being posted to Canada, where he served as an instructor. After a spell as a staff officer at Bomber Command, and further instructional duties, Grindon returned to operations with No 106 Sqn in July 1944 as a flight commander. Within five weeks he had been promoted to wing commander and taken charge of No 630 Sqn. Grindon earned a DSO for his leadership of this unit in July 1945.

TIGER FORCE

Although the conflict in Europe was clearly at an end, the war against Japan still raged, so preparations had begun in December 1944 for the formation of a Far East bombing force (known as Tiger Force) that would supplement the USAAF assault on the Japanese mainland. The intention was for RAF units to initially operate from Burma, with both Nos 9 and 617 Sqns using *Grandslam* and *Tallboy* in a low-level tactical support role.

8 May 1945 brought the day the whole world had been waiting for when 'Victory in Europe', or VE Day, was officially declared. Spontaneous parties broke out across Britain, but there was little time for celebrating in the RAF, as it immediately despatched hundreds of aircraft on flights to the continent to repatriate former Allied PoWs back to the UK in Operation *Exodus*. Five crews from No 617 Sqn took part in the latter on VE Day itself, and it continued over the following week, interspersed with continental cross-country flights that were known as 'Cook's Tours', which gave the groundcrews an opportunity to see at first hand the result of five years of bombing operations.

B I (Special) PD119/YZ-J airborne on 18 May 1945. As the half-black/half-white tail scheme intended for identification purposes had proved unsuccessful, the unit reverted to overall black on the outer surfaces, which remained until the end of the war. Clearly seen is another item of daylight identification – the squadron code letters painted across the tail surfaces (*IWM Neg No MH30793*)

A photograph of the coastal batteries at Heligoland after they had been bombed by No 617 Sqn on the unit's penultimate raid of the war, on 19 April 1945. The photograph was taken by Flg Off Ray Wilkinson from the rear turret of PD371/KC-W during a 'Cook's Tour' on 16 May 1945, with the aircraft being flown by Flt Lt Ian Marshall. The large craters to the left were caused by the last *Grandslams* dropped during the war (*Ray Wilkinson*)

It was during one of these that Lt Bill Adams (a USAAF pilot serving with No 617 Sqn) suffered an engine failure in B I (Special) PD139/YZ-L and had to force-land his bomber near Brunswick, fortunately without any injuries.

At the end of the month No 617's C Flight was despatched to RAF Mildenhall to become part of No 15 Sqn, taking its B I (Special) Lancasters with it. This unit was to undertake bombing trials with both *Grandslam* and *Tallboy* against captured fortified targets such as the U-boat pens at Farge and Heligoland as part of Operation *Front Line*. Other sorties were also flown alongside trials conducted by the USAAF as part of Operation *Ruby*.

Meanwhile, back at Woodhall Spa, the rest of No 617 Sqn was preparing for Tiger Force, starting with a move to RAF Waddington

B I (Special) Lancasters PD129/YZ-O and PD118/YZ-M in company with standard B I NG489/KC-M on 18 May 1945, photographed from B I (Special) PD116/YZ-A, flown by Flt Lt Bob Horsley. The differences in the two variants, the colour schemes and style of codes are particularly noticeable (*IWM Neg No MH30795*)

PD139/YZ-L on its belly near Brunswick, in Germany, after being crash-landed by Lt Bill Adams during a 'Cook's Tour' on 16 May 1945. This was the last B I (Special) made, and it was scrapped where it lay soon after this photograph was taken (*Tom Collins*)

on 17 June 1945. Crews flew many long-range navigation exercises around the UK, often of ten hours or more duration, replicating what they expected to encounter in the Far East.

At the same time the unit began to take delivery of a brand new batch of Lancasters, designated B VII (FE) (for 'Far East'), which were more suited for operations in extreme heat and over long distances. Notable differences between No 617 Sqn's previous aircraft and the new Lancasters included a Martin electric mid-upper turret, situated further forward of the original position, and a Frazer-Nash FN 82 rear turret (both turrets being fitted with a pair of powerful 0.5-in Browning machine guns).

The B VII (FE) also boasted up-rated engines and a striking new paint scheme of white upper and black undersurfaces, as the usual European scheme of dark earth and dark green uppersurfaces and black (night) or grey (day) undersides was considered inappropriate for operations in the Far East.

The force was due to be deployed by 20 November 1945, with No 617 Sqn being based on the island of Okinawa, rather than in Burma. Its job would be to bomb bridges connecting Kyushu with the Japanese mainland, thus preventing enemy reinforcements from occupying the area when American forces invaded.

Training continued throughout July and into August, but before any elements of the squadron had left Britain, news was received of the dropping of the first atomic bomb on Hiroshima on 6 August, followed three days later by a similar attack on Nagasaki. The world saw for the first time the truly devastating power of this new type of weapon, which brought about the formal declaration of surrender from the Japanese on 15 August, on what was subsequently termed 'Victory over Japan' or VJ Day. With World War 2 finally at an end, the need for Tiger Force had gone, and it was officially cancelled on 2 September 1945.

9 August had also brought a new commanding officer to No 617 Sqn, Wg Cdr Charles Fothergill being charged with seeing the unit's transition to peace.

AFTERWARDS

The end of the war saw a dramatic reduction in the size of the RAF, with many squadrons being disbanded altogether. This was not to be No 617 Sqn's fate, however, and as Christmas approached the unit received word that it was to fly to Digri, in India, in the New Year, where it would be based for four months. No 9 Sqn accompanied the unit to the Far East, being based at nearby Salbani.

As India prepared for independence, there was some concern that civil disturbances may erupt, marring the negotiations and endangering British forces as they prepared to leave, so the two units remained on standby should any emergency arise. In Bombay, some units of the Indian Navy did indeed mutiny, but thankfully no major incident occurred, and the squadrons' time on the continent was trouble-free. However, before returning to the UK the Lancaster units were invited to participate in the victory celebrations in Delhi in April 1946, and they did not disappoint, exciting the crowds with a low-level flypast by six Lancasters.

Once back in the UK, No 617 Sqn began to re-equip with the new Avro Lincoln – a larger version of the Lancaster – at its new RAF Binbrook home.

Lancaster VII (FE) NX791/KC-E at Digri, in India, during No 617 Sqn's four-month stay on the continent. The Martin mid-upper turret fitted to the Mk VII Lancaster can be seen further forward of the usual position, while the striking black and white colour scheme, applied to all aircraft destined for Tiger Force, is still in use almost eight months after the planned force was scrapped (*Peter Green*)

A six-Lancaster flypast over Delhi in April 1946 to mark India's victory celebrations and the end of No 617 Sqn's stay on the continent (*Peter Green*)

OPERATION *GUZZLE*

Although discussions had continued throughout 1943 and much of 1944, no further operations using *Upkeep* had been carried out, and by December 1944 it was confirmed that none were likely in the immediate future. By then the remaining 'Dambuster' aircraft had been flown to RAF Lossiemouth for storage, although they were to be available at seven days notice, later extended to 21. During routine inspections of the surviving mines, however, one was found to be in so poor a state that it was deemed unsafe. As standard aircraft could not drop them, Bomber Command issued an instruction on 26 March 1945 for one of the modified types to be prepared and flown to Woodhall Spa to dispose of it. ED933 was the aircraft selected, and after dropping the mine in the sea during a flight in early April, the bomber returned to Lossiemouth at the end of the month.

By the start of 1946 the rest of the mines were showing signs of deterioration too, with the contents starting to leak and the casings beginning to corrode. Since June 1945 the RAF had been tasked with dumping thousands of tons of surplus bombs in the sea in Operation *Wastage*, and as part of this procedure, detailed instructions were drawn up for the disposal of the rest of the *Upkeep* mines under the codename of Operation *Gnat*.

Provisional arrangements were made in early February 1946 for three 'Dambuster' Lancasters (ED906, ED909 and ED932) to be refurbished at Lossiemouth and then flown to Scampton for this task, which was expected to commence in late May. They were officially allocated to No 61 Sqn for the duration, which in turn was told to relinquish three of its own aircraft. However, like No 617 Sqn, it too was converting to the Lincoln, and so it merely gave up its Lancasters as

Wg Cdr Gibson's 'Dambusting' Lancaster ED932, seen at RAF Scampton in the spring of 1947, having completed its work disposing of surplus *Upkeep* mines in Operation *Guzzle*. The aircraft carries the codes YF-C of the Station Flight in white. It was struck off charge in July that year and scrapped whilst still at Scampton (*Peter Green*)

planned. The crews were drawn from Nos 9, 61, 101 and 617 Sqns, thus allowing all four units to continue with their conversion to the new bomber type. Finding aircrew had not been a problem for the RAF, but locating armourers familiar with the weapon was no easy task, as most had now left the service.

By the time the aircraft were finally ready the codename had unaccountably changed to Operation *Guzzle*. ED909 arrived at Scampton on 13 August 1946, followed by the remaining two Lancasters a fortnight later. Despite the work done at Lossiemouth, considerable refurbishment was still needed, however. Indeed, ED932 required a complete engine change, as all four of its Merlins were time-expired, and the three aircraft were still fitted with *Gee* and VHF radio.

Operation *Guzzle* commenced on 22 August 1946 with a drop from ED909 (uncoded at the time), flown by Flt Lt Steve Nunns of No 617 Sqn. More flights were made throughout the month and into September. Although the mines were carried in the same way as they had originally been in 1943, they were dropped from around 10,000 ft without being spun or fused. Even so, several crews reported seeing explosions as they hit the sea.

The serviceability of the three aircraft plagued *Guzzle* throughout, with a drop from ED909 being cancelled on 16 September because of a faulty bomb release. On another occasion Flg Off Steve Norris had to jettison his mine early after a fire broke out on board, rendering his wireless equipment useless. In early November Norris had another hair-raising flight when he struck the runway during take-off in ED932 whilst trying to avoid a large flock of birds. The undercarriage took the brunt of the force, but Norris carried on, flying the entire six-and-a-half-hour trip with the starboard undercarriage leg only partly retracted. As he returned to Scampton emergency air was used to lower the wheels,

ED906, the aircraft flown by Flt Lt David Maltby to the Dams in May 1943, is seen parked on the grass at RAF Scampton in the spring of 1947. After being used in Operation *Guzzle*, it was given the code YF-A of the Station Flight and its serial was painted under the wing in white. Immediately behind the aircraft can be seen Hanger 1, and to the right of that, Hanger 2, the home of No 617 Sqn when initially formed at Scampton four years earlier

Mick Martin's Dambuster ED909 being broken up at Scampton in July 1947. In June 1944 it had been used on the operation to the Saumar Railway Tunnel, fitted with H2S and carrying a load of 1000-lb bombs. Also flown during Operation *Guzzle*, the veteran bomber was struck off charge in July 1947 and scrapped where it stood

and although a safe landing was made, the damage was sufficient enough to see the aircraft declared Category AC (repair by contractors). This left just ED909 and ED906 to drop the remaining mines.

The rest of the *Guzzle* flights were made in December 1946, with the last performed on the 21st. Having disposed of all the mines, the three Lancasters were allocated to the Station Flight at Scampton with the new codes YF. They remained here until July 1947, when the bombers were struck off charge and broken up, having first had their 'Dambuster' equipment removed. The others had met a similar fate a few months earlier. *Guzzle* had seen No 617 Sqn come full circle from its formation almost exactly four years before.

In January 1952 No 617 Sqn moved into the jet age, swapping its Lincoln B 2s for Canberra B 2s, which it took to Malaya in late June 1955 to quell unrest by communist forces. This deployment was the unit's first operationally for ten years, and upon its return to the UK on 1 December 1955 the squadron received news that it was to be disbanded two weeks later as part of the continuing policy of reducing the RAF's overall size. This period in the wilderness did not last long, however, as No 617 Sqn was reformed on 1 May 1958 at its original base of RAF Scampton with the Avro Vulcan B 1 bomber. In 1961 the unit echoed its wartime days by becoming the first squadron to be equipped with the *Blue Steel* stand-off weapon – a rocket-powered thermo-nuclear missile that could be released miles from a target, and a forerunner to the long-range missiles of today.

No 617 Sqn was disbanded for a second time on 31 December 1981, but it had already been earmarked for reformation on 1 January 1983, this time with the new Tornado GR 1 strike aircraft. Having earned more battle honours over Iraq in 1991 and 2003, the unit currently flies the Tornado GR 4 from RAF Lossiemouth, in Scotland, in the air interdiction, close air support, ground attack, reconnaissance and suppression of enemy air defences roles.

APPENDICES

APPENDIX 1

No 617 SQN TARGETS

1943

The Dams	16-17 May
Aquata Scriva (Italy)	15 July
San Polo D'Enza (Italy)	15 July
Leghorn (Italy)	24 July
Milan (Italy)	29 July
Turin (Italy)	29 July
Genoa (Italy)	29 July
Bologna (Italy)	29 July
Dortmund-Ems Canal	15 September
Antheor Viaduct	16 September
Antheor Viaduct	11 November
Doullons	10 December
Flixecourt	16 December
Liege	20 December
Pas de Calais	22 December
Flixecourt	30 December

1944

Pas de Calais	4 January
Pas de Calais	21 January
Pas de Calais	25 January
Limoges	8 February
Antheor Viaduct	12 February
Albert	2 March
St Etienne	4 March
St Etienne	10 March
Woippy	15 March
Clermont Ferrand	16 March
Bergerac	18 March
Angouleme	20 March
Lyons	23 March
Lyons	25 March
Lyons	29 March
Toulouse	5 April
St Cyr	10 April
Juvisy	18 April
La Chapelle	20 April
Brunswick	22 April
Munich	24 April

Milan (Italy)	24 April
Mailly-Le-Camp	3 May
Operation *Taxable*	5 June
Saumar Tunnel	8 June
Le Havre	14 June
Boulogne	15 June
Watten	19 June
Wizernes	20 June
Wizernes	22 June
Wizernes	24 June
Siracourt	25 June
Creil	4 July
Mimoyecques	6 July
Wizernes	17 July
Wizernes	20 July
Watten	25 July
Rilly La Montagne	31 July
Siracourt	1 August
Etaples	4 August
Brest	5 August
Lorient	6 August
Lorient	7 August
La Pallice	9 August
La Pallice	11 August
Brest	12 August
Gueydon (ship) Brest	13 August
Gueydon (ship) Brest	14 August
La Pallice	16 August
La Pallice	18 August
Ijmuiden	24 August
Brest	27 August
Tirpitz (ship)	11 September
Dortmund-Ems Canal	23 September
Westkappel Sea Wall	3 October
Kembs Canal	7 October
Tirpitz (ship)	29 October
Tirpitz (ship)	12 November
Urft Dam	8 December
Urft Dam	11 December
Ijmuiden	15 December

117

Politz	21 December	Bielefeld	14 March
Rotterdam	29 December	Arnsberg	15 March
Ijmuiden	30 December	Arnsberg	19 March
		Dreys	21 March
1945		Nienburg	22 March
Oslo	31 December-	Bremen	23 March
	1 January	Farge	27 March
Bergen (Norway)	12 January	Ijmuiden	6 April
Pootershaven	3 February	Ijmuiden	7 April
Bielefeld	6 February	Hamburg U-boat pens	9 April
Ijmuiden	8 February	*Prinz Eugen & Lützow* (ships)	13 April
Bielefeld	14 February	*Lützow* (ship)	15 April
Bielefeld	22 February	*Lützow* (ship)	16 April
Dortmund-Ems Canal	24 February	Heligoland	19 April
Bielefeld	9 March	Berchtesgarden	25 April
Bielefeld	13 March		

APPENDIX 2

SQUADRON COMMANDERS

Wg Cdr Guy Gibson VC, DSO, DFC	21/3/45 to 3/8/43	Wg Cdr James Tait DSO, DFC	12/7/44 to 29/12/44
Wg Cdr George Holden DSO, DFC	3/8/43 to 16/9/43	Grp Capt John Fauquier DSO, DFC	29/12/44 to 28/4/45
Sqn Ldr Harold Martin (Temp) DSO, DFC	16/9/43 to 10/11/43	Wg Cdr John Grindon DSO, DFC	28/4/45 to 9/8/45
Wg Cdr Leonard Cheshire VC, DSO, DFC	10/11/43 to 12/7/44	Wg Cdr Charles Fothergill	9/8/45 to 4/46

APPENDIX 3

BASES

RAF Scampton	21/3/43 to 30/8/43	RAF Waddington	17/6/45 to 31/12/45
RAF Coningsby	30/8/43 to 9/1/44	Digri (India)	31/12/45 to 15/4/46
RAF Woodhall Spa	9/1/44 to 17/6/45	RAF Binbrook	15/4/46 to 1/8/46

APPENDIX 4

BATTLE HONOURS

The Dams 1943	Channel and North Sea 1944/45
France and Germany 1944/45	Biscay Ports 1944
Fortress of Europe 1944	*Tirpitz* 1944
Normandy 1944	German Ports 1945

APPENDIX 5

AIRCRAFT LOSSES

16-17 May 1943 – Operations (Dams Raid)

Lancaster Type 464 Provisioning ED864/AJ-B
Crashed near Marbeck, Germany

Pilot	Flt Lt W Astell	Killed
Flight Engineer	Sgt J Kinnear	Killed
Navigator	Plt Off F A Wile RCAF	Killed
Wireless Operator	WO A Garshowitz RCAF	Killed
Bomb Aimer	Flg Off D Hopkinson	Killed
Front Gunner	Flt Sgt F A Garbas RCAF	Killed
Rear Gunner	Sgt R Bolitho	Killed

Lancaster Type 464 Provisioning ED865/AJ-S
Crashed at Gilze Rijen, Holland

Pilot	Plt Off L J Burpee RCAF	Killed
Flight Engineer	Sgt G Pegler	Killed
Navigator	Sgt T Jaye	Killed
Wireless Operator	Plt Off L G Weller	Killed
Bomb Aimer	WO J L Arthur RCAF	Killed
Front Gunner	Sgt W C A Long	Killed
Rear Gunner	WO J G Brady RCAF	Killed

Lancaster Type 464 Provisioning ED887/AJ-A
Crashed into the North Sea off Dutch coast

Pilot	Sqn Ldr H M Young	Killed
Flight Engineer	Sgt D T Horsfall	Killed
Navigator	Flt Sgt C W Roberts	Killed
Wireless Operator	Sgt L W Nichols	Killed
Bomb Aimer	Flg Off V S MacCausland RCAF	Killed
Front Gunner	Sgt G A Yeo	Killed
Rear Gunner	Sgt W Ibbotson	Killed

Lancaster Type 464 Provisioning ED910/AJ-C
Crashed near Hamm, Germany

Pilot	Plt Off W Ottley	Killed
Flight Engineer	Sgt R Marsden	Killed
Navigator	Flg Off J K Barrett	Killed
Wireless Operator	Sgt J Guterman	Killed
Bomb Aimer	Flt Sgt T B Johnston	Killed
Front Gunner	Sgt H J Strange	Killed
Rear Gunner	Sgt F Tees	PoW

Lancaster Type 464 Provisioning ED925/AJ-M
Crashed at Ostönnen, Germany

Pilot	Flt Lt J V Hopgood	Killed
Flight Engineer	Sgt C Brennan	Killed
Navigator	Flg Off K Earnshaw RCAF	Killed
Wireless Operator	Sgt J W Minchin	Killed
Bomb Aimer	Plt Off J W Fraser RCAF	PoW
Front Gunner	Plt Off H F G Gregory	Killed
Rear Gunner	Flg Off A F Burcher RAAF	PoW

Lancaster Type 464 Provisioning ED927/AJ-E
Crashed at Haldern, Germany

Pilot	Flt Lt R N G Barlow RAAF	Killed
Flight Engineer	Plt Off S L Whillis	Killed
Navigator	Flg Off P S Burgess	Killed
Wireless Operator	Flg Off C R Williams RAAF	Killed
Bomb Aimer	Plt Off A Gillespie	Killed
Front Gunner	Flg Off H S Glinz RCAF	Killed
Rear Gunner	Sgt J R G Liddell	Killed

Lancaster Type 464 Provisioning ED934/AJ-K
Crashed in the Waddenzee, off Dutch coast

Pilot	Plt Off V W Byers RCAF	Killed
Flight Engineer	Sgt A J Taylor	Killed
Navigator	Flg Off J H Warner	Killed
Wireless Operator	Sgt J Wilkinson	Killed
Bomb Aimer	Plt Off A N Whitaker	Killed
Front Gunner	Sgt C M Jarvie	Killed
Rear Gunner	Flt Sgt J McDowell RCAF	Killed

Lancaster Type 464 Provisioning ED937/AJ-Z
Crashed at Emmerich, Germany

Pilot	Sqn Ldr H E Maudslay	Killed
Flight Engineer	Sgt J Marriott	Killed
Navigator	Flg Off R A Urquhart RCAF	Killed
Wireless Operator	WO A P Cottam RCAF	Killed
Bomb Aimer	Plt Off M J D Fuller	Killed
Front Gunner	Flg Off W J Tytherleigh	Killed
Rear Gunner	Sgt N R Burrows	Killed

6 June 1943 – Training

Lancaster B III EE145/AJ-T
Crashed upon landing at RAF Scampton

Pilot	Flt Lt J L Munro RNZAF	Uninjured
Flight Engineer	Sgt F Appleby	Uninjured
Navigator	Flg Off G Rumbles	Uninjured
Wireless Operator	WO P E Pigeon	Uninjured
Bomb Aimer	Sgt J H Clay	Uninjured
Mid-Upper Gunner	Sgt W Howarth	Uninjured
Rear Gunner	WO H A Weeks	Uninjured
Passenger	Cpl Lees	Uninjured

5 August 1943 – Training

Lancaster Type 464 Provisioning ED765/AJ-M

Crashed at Ashley Walk Bombing Range, Hampshire

Pilot	Flt Lt W A Kellaway	Injured
Flight Engineer	Sgt E Owen	Injured
Navigator	Plt Off N R Drury	Injured
Bomb Aimer	Flt Sgt S W Harris	Injured
Front Gunner	Sgt G W Horsfield	Injured
Rear Gunner	Flt Sgt E C Temple	Injured

(only six crew aboard)

15 September 1943 – Operations (Dortmund-Ems Canal)

Lancaster B III JA981/KC-J

Crashed into the North Sea after raid was aborted

Pilot	Sqn Ldr D J H Maltby	Killed
Flight Engineer	Sgt W Hatton	Killed
Navigator	Flt Sgt V Nicholson	Killed
Wireless Operator	Flt Sgt A J Stone	Killed
Bomb Aimer	Plt Off J Fort	Killed
Front Gunner	Sgt V Hill	Killed
Mid-Upper Gunner	WO J L Welch	Killed
Rear Gunner	Sgt H T Simmonds	Killed

16 September 1943 – Operations (Dortmund-Ems Canal)

Lancaster B III EE130/KC-A

Crashed near Bergeshövede, Germany

Pilot	Flt Lt R A P Allsebrook	Killed
Flight Engineer	Flt Sgt P Moore	Killed
Navigator	Plt Off N A Botting	Killed
Wireless Operator	Flg Off J M Grant	Killed
Bomb Aimer	Flt Sgt R B M Lulham	Killed
Front Gunner	Sgt I G Jones	Killed
Mid-Upper Gunner	Flt Sgt W Walker	Killed
Rear Gunner	Flt Sgt S Hitchen	Killed

Lancaster B III EE144/KC-S

Crashed near Altendorf, Germany

Pilot	Sqn Ldr G W Holden	Killed
Flight Engineer	Sgt D J D Powell	Killed
Navigator	Flt Lt H T Taerum RCAF	Killed
Wireless Operator	Flt Lt R E G Hutchison	Killed
Bomb Aimer	Flg Off F M Spafford RAAF	Killed
Front Gunner	Plt Off G A Deering RCAF	Killed
Mid-Upper Gunner	Flg Off H J Pringle	Killed
Rear Gunner	Plt Off T A Meikle	Killed

Lancaster B III JA874/KC-E

Crashed at Bramsche, Germany

Pilot	Plt Off W G Divall	Killed
Flight Engineer	Sgt E C A Blake	Killed
Navigator	Flg Off D W Warwick RCAF	Killed
Wireless Operator	Flt Sgt J S Simpson	Killed
Bomb Aimer	Flt Sgt R C McArthur	Killed
Front Gunner	Sgt A A Williams	Killed
Mid-Upper Gunner	Sgt G S Miles	Killed
Rear Gunner	Sgt D Allatson	Killed

Lancaster B III JA898/KC-X

Crashed near Recke, Germany

Pilot	Flt Lt H S Wilson	Killed
Flight Engineer	Plt Off T W Johnson	Killed
Navigator	Flg Off J A Rodger	Killed
Wireless Operator	WO L Mieyette RCAF	Killed
Bomb Aimer	Flg Off G H Coles RCAF	Killed
Front Gunner	Flt Sgt T H Payne	Killed
Mid-Upper Gunner	Sgt C M Knox	Killed
Rear Gunner	Flt Sgt E Hornby	Killed

Lancaster B III JB144/KC-N

Crashed at Den Hamm, Holland

Pilot	Flt Lt L G Knight RAAF	Killed
Flight Engineer	Plt Off R E Grayston	PoW
Navigator	Plt Off H S Hobday	Evaded
Wireless Operator	Plt Off R G Kellow RAAF	Evaded
Bomb Aimer	Flg Off E C Johnson	Evaded
Front Gunner	Flt Sgt F E Sutherland RCAF	Evaded
Mid-Upper Gunner	Sgt L C Woollard	Evaded
Rear Gunner	Flt Sgt H E O'Brien RCAF	PoW

18 November 1943 – Transit Flight to UK from North Africa

Lancaster B III ED735/KC-R

Ditched in the Bay of Biscay

Pilot	Flt Lt E E G Youseman	Killed
Flight Engineer	Plt Off S J Whittingham	Killed
Navigator	Plt Off L Plishka RCAF	Killed
Wireless Operator	Flg Off W C Grimes	Killed
Bomb Aimer	Flt Sgt R Florence RNZAF	Killed
Mid-Upper Gunner	Plt Off A M Laughland RCAF	Killed
Rear Gunner	WO J B O'Grady RCAF	Killed

10 December 1943 – Operations (Arms drop, France)

Lancaster Type 464 Provisioning ED825/KC-E

Crashed at Doullens, France

Pilot	Flg Off G H Weeden RCAF	Killed
Flight Engineer	Sgt A W Richardson	Killed
Navigator	Plt Off R N Jones	Killed
Wireless Operator	Flt Sgt R G Howell	Killed
Bomb Aimer	WO E J Walters RCAF	Killed
Front Gunner	Sgt B Robinson	Killed
Rear Gunner	WO R Cummings RCAF	Killed

Lancaster Type 464 Provisioning ED886/KC-O

Crashed at Terramesnil, France

Pilot	WO G Bull	PoW
Flight Engineer	Sgt O Wiltshire	PoW
Navigator	Sgt C C Chamberlain	PoW
Wireless Operator	Sgt J M Stewart	Killed
Bomb Aimer	Flt Sgt N Batey	PoW
Front Gunner	Sgt J H McWilliams	PoW
Rear Gunner	Flt Sgt R Thorpe RCAF	Killed

21 December 1943 – Operations (Liege, Belgium)

Lancaster B I DV398/KC-Z

Crashed near Merbes-le-Château, Belgium

Pilot	Flt Lt G Rice	PoW
Flight Engineer	Flt Sgt E C Smith	Killed
Navigator	Flg Off R McFarlane	Killed
Wireless Operator	WO C B Gowrie RCAF	Killed
Bomb Aimer	WO J W Thrasher RCAF	Killed
Mid-Upper Gunner	Flt Sgt T W Maynard	Killed
Rear Gunner	Flt Sgt S Burns	Killed

20 January 1944 – Training

Lancaster Type 464 Provisioning ED918/AJ-F

Crashed at Snettisham Beach, near Kings Lynn, Norfolk

Pilot	Flt Lt T V O'Shaughnessy	Killed
Navigator	Flg Off A D Holding	Killed
Wireless Operator	Plt Off A J Ward	Injured
Bomb Aimer	Flg Off G A Kendrick	Injured

(only four crew aboard)

13 February 1944 – Transit Flight to Base

Lancaster B I DV382/KC-J

Crashed at Waltham Down, Sussex

Pilot	Sqn Ldr W R Suggitt RCAF	Killed
Flight Engineer	Flt Sgt J Pulford	Killed
Navigator	Plt Off J I Gordon RAAF	Killed
Wireless Operator	Plt Off S G Hall	Killed
Bomb Aimer	Flg Off N J Davidson RCAF	Killed
Mid-Upper Gunner	Flt Sgt J P Riches	Killed

Rear Gunner	Flg Off J McB Dempster	Killed
Passenger	Sqn Ldr T W Lloyd	Killed

24 April 1944 – Operations (Munich, Germany)

Lancaster B I DV394/KC-M

Crashed near Aichstetten, Germany

Pilot	Flt Lt J L Cooper	PoW
Flight Engineer	Flg Off T W Clarkson	PoW
Navigator	Flt Lt F E Drew	PoW
Wireless Operator	Flg Off J H Lepine RCAF	PoW
Bomb Aimer	Flg Off G H Harden	Killed
Mid-Upper Gunner	Flg Off A E Pelly	PoW
Rear Gunner	Flg Off F J Tucker	PoW

24 June 1944 – Operations (Wizernes, France)

Lancaster B I DV403/KC-G

Crashed at Leulinghem, France

Pilot	Flt Lt J A Edward	Killed
Flight Engineer	Flg Off L W J King	Killed
Navigator	Flg Off L T Pritchard RCAF	PoW
Wireless Operator	Flt Sgt G A Hobbs	PoW
Bomb Aimer	Flt Sgt J Brook	PoW
Front Gunner	Plt Off J I Johnstone RCAF	Killed
Mid-Upper Gunner	Flt Sgt S Isherwood	Killed
Rear Gunner	WO T W P Price RCAF	Killed

14 July 1944 – Transit Flight

Lancaster B I ME560/KC-G

Crashed upon landing at RAF Woodhall Spa

Pilot	Flg Off M L Hamilton	Uninjured
Flight Engineer	Flt Sgt J T Rooke	Uninjured
Navigator	Plt Off J T Jackson	Uninjured
Wireless Operator	Flt Sgt R C Thompson	Uninjured
Bomb Aimer	Flg Off F C Atkinson RCAF	Uninjured
Mid-Upper Gunner	Flt Sgt D Hamilton	Uninjured
Rear Gunner	WO T J McLean	Uninjured
Passenger	Flg Off R T Duck	Uninjured
Passenger	Flt Lt R M S Matthews	Uninjured
Passenger	Unknown Medical Orderly	Uninjured

28 July 1944 – Training

Lancaster Type 464 Provisioning ED936/AJ-H

Crashed upon landing at RAF Woodhall Spa

Crew unknown, no fatalities or serious injuries reported

31 July 1944 – Operations (Rilly-La-Montagne, France)

Lancaster B I ME557/KC-S

Crashed at Germaine, France

Pilot	Flt Lt W Reid	PoW
Flight Engineer	Flt Sgt D G W Stewart	Killed
Navigator	Flg Off J O Peltier RCAF	Killed
Wireless Operator	Flg Off D Luker	PoW
Bomb Aimer	Plt Off L G Rolton	Killed
Mid-Upper Gunner	Flt Sgt A A Holt	Killed
Rear Gunner	WO J W Hutton	Killed

5 August 1944 – Operations (Brest, France)

Lancaster B III JB139/KC-V

Crashed into Douarnenez Bay, France

Pilot	Flt Lt D H Cheney RCAF	Evaded
Flight Engineer	Flt Sgt J Rosher	Evaded
Navigator	Plt Off R Welch	Killed
Wireless Operator	Flt Sgt R H Pool	Killed
Bomb Aimer	Flt Sgt L Curtis	PoW
Mid-Upper Gunner	WO K R Porter RCAF	Evaded
Rear Gunner	Plt Off W N Wait	Killed

7 August 1944 – Training (Wainfleet Bombing Range)

Mosquito FB VI NT202/N

Crashed on the Wainfleet Bombing Range

Pilot	Flg Off W A Duffy RCAF	Killed
Navigator	Flt Lt P Ingleby	Killed

11 September 1944 – Operations (*Tirpitz*, Norway)

Lancaster B I ME559/KC-Y

Crashed upon landing at Kegostrov

Pilot	Sqn Ldr D R C Wyness	Uninjured
Flight Engineer	Flg Off J S Naylor	Uninjured
Navigator	Flt Lt R H Williams	Uninjured
Wireless Operator	Flg Off D C Shea	Uninjured
Bomb Aimer	Flg Off H W Honig	Uninjured
Front Gunner	Flt Sgt T Horrocks	Uninjured
Rear Gunner	Plt Off G E Cansell	Uninjured

Lancaster B III EE131/KC-B

Crashed upon landing at Molotovsk

Pilot	Flg Off I S Ross RAAF	Uninjured
Flight Engineer	Sgt W Walter	Uninjured
Navigator	Flt Sgt A Jackson	Uninjured

Wireless Operator	Flt Sgt K Jenkinson	Uninjured
Bomb Aimer	Flt Sgt E G Tilby	Uninjured
Front Gunner	Flt Sgt R D Griffiths	Uninjured
Rear Gunner	Plt Off A F McKellar	Uninjured

17 September 1944 – Operations (Return from Russia)

Lancaster B III PB416/KC-V

Crashed in Norway

Pilot	Flg Off F Levy	Killed
Flight Engineer	Sgt P W Groom	Killed
Navigator	Flg Off C L Fox	Killed
Wireless Operator	Flt Sgt G M McGuire	Killed
Bomb Aimer	Flt Sgt E E S Peck	Killed
Front Gunner	Plt Off A F McNally RCAF	Killed
Rear Gunner	Flt Sgt D G Thomas	Killed
Passenger	Flg Off J F Naylor	Killed
Passenger	D C Shea	Killed

24 September 1944 – Operations (Dortmund-Ems Canal, Germany)

Lancaster B I NF923/KC-M

Crashed near Lochem, Holland

Pilot	Flt Lt G S Stout	Killed
Flight Engineer	Plt Off A W Benting	Killed
Navigator	Flg Off C E M Graham	Killed
Wireless Operator	Flg Off R J Allen	PoW
Bomb Aimer	Flg Off W A Rupert RCAF	Evaded
Mid-Upper Gunner	Flt Sgt P L Whittaker	PoW
Rear Gunner	Flg Off R H Petch	Evaded

7 October 1944 – Operations (Kembs Barrage, Germany)

Lancaster B I NG180/KC-S

Crashed into the Rhine, Germany

Pilot	Sqn Ldr D R C Wyness	Killed
Flight Engineer	Flt Sgt T J Hurdiss	Killed
Navigator	Flt Lt R H Williams	Killed
Wireless Operator	Flg Off B J Hosie RNZAF	Killed
Bomb Aimer	Flg Off H W Honig	Killed
Mid-Upper Gunner	Flt Sgt T Horrocks	Killed
Rear Gunner	Flg Off G E Cansell	Killed

Lancaster B III LM482/KC-Q

Crashed at Efringen-Kirchen, Germany

Pilot	Flt Lt C J G Howard	Killed
Flight Engineer	Plt Off F C Hawkins	Killed
Navigator	Flt Lt T J Tate	Killed

Wireless Operator	Plt Off R D Lucan	Killed
Bomb Aimer	Plt Off E A Hartley	Killed
Front Gunner	Flg Off D T Watkins	Killed
Mid-Upper Gunner	WO P E Woods	Killed
Rear Gunner	Flt Sgt H G Clarke	Killed

29 October 1944 – Operations (*Tirpitz*, Norway)

Lancaster B I NF920/KC-E

Crashed Porjus, Sweden

Pilot	Flg Off D W Carey	Interned
Flight Engineer	Flt Sgt L Franks	Interned
Navigator	Plt Off A M McKie	Interned
Wireless Operator	Plt Off D H MacLennan	Interned
Bomb Aimer	Flt Sgt A E Young	Interned
Rear Gunner	Flg Off G A Witherick	Interned

(only six crew aboard)

22 December 1944 – Operations (Politz, Germany)

Lancaster B I ME561/KC-T

Crashed on approach to RAF Ludford Magna, Lincolnshire

Pilot	Flg Off A W Joplin RNZAF	Injured
Flight Engineer	Sgt F L Tilley	Injured
Navigator	Flt Sgt C B R Fish	Injured
Wireless Operator	Flt Sgt G Cooke	Injured
Bomb Aimer	Flg Off A J Walker	Killed
Mid-Upper Gunner	Flg Off R B Yates	Killed
Rear Gunner	Flt Sgt J T Thompson	Injured

12 January 1945 – Operations (Bergen, Norway)

Lancaster B I NF992/KC-B

Ditched off Norwegian coast

Pilot	Flg Off I S Ross RAAF	Killed
Flight Engineer	Flt Sgt W Walter	Killed
Navigator	WO S R Anderson	Killed
Wireless Operator	Flg Off M Ellwood	Killed
Bomb Aimer	Plt Off E G Tilby	Killed
Front Gunner	Flt Sgt L D Griffiths	Killed
Rear Gunner	Flt Sgt A F McKellar	Killed

Lancaster B I PD233/KC-G

Crashed at Lille Landon, Norway

Pilot	Flt Lt J H Pryor	PoW
Flight Engineer	Flt Sgt A L Winston	PoW
Navigator	Flg Off H Ellis	PoW
Wireless Operator	Plt Off A Hepworth	PoW

Bomb Aimer	Flg Off G A Kendrick	Killed
Front Gunner	Flt Lt E N Armstrong	PoW
Rear Gunner	WO E C Temple	PoW

21 March 1945 – Operations (Arbergen Viaduct, Germany)

Lancaster B I (Special) PD117/YZ-L

Crashed at Okel, Germany

Pilot	Flt Lt B A Gumbley RNZAF	Killed
Flight Engineer	Flg Off E A Barnett	Killed
Navigator	Flg Off K Gill	Killed
Bomb Aimer	Flt Lt J C Randon	Killed
Rear Gunner	Flg Off G Bell	Killed

(only five crew aboard)

5 April 1945 – Ferry Flight (to RAF Lossiemouth)

Lancaster B I PB415/KC-O

Crashed at RAF Lossiemouth

| Pilot | Lt W Adams USAAF | Uninjured |
| Navigator | Plt Off J Langston | Uninjured |

(only two crew aboard)

16 April 1945 – Operations (Swinemünde, Germany)

Lancaster B I NG228/KC-V

Crashed at Swinemunde

Pilot	Sqn Ldr J L Powell	Killed
Flight Engineer	Flt Sgt H W Felton	Killed
Navigator	Flt Lt M T Clarke	Killed
Wireless Operator	Plt Off K A J Hewitt	Killed
Bomb Aimer	Flg Off A L Heath	Killed
Mid-Upper Gunner	Flt Sgt W Knight	Killed
Rear Gunner	Flg Off J Watson	Killed

16 May 1945 – Continental Cross Country ('Cook's Tour')

Lancaster B I (Special) PD139/YZ-L

Crashed near Brunswick

Pilot	Lt W Adam USAAF	Uninjured
Flight Engineer	Flt Sgt A Swann	Uninjured
Navigator	Plt Off T H Collins	Uninjured
Bomb Aimer	Flt Lt R K Foulkes	Uninjured
Rear Gunner	Flt Lt R Girvan	Uninjured
Unknown Passengers		Uninjured

(only five crew aboard)

COLOUR PLATES

1

Lancaster B III ED763/AJ-D, Scampton, April 1943

ED763 was initially allocated to No 467 Sqn in late March 1943. However, it remained with the unit for little more than a week (and took part in no operations) before being flown to RAF Scampton on 2 April to become one of the original ten Lancasters given to No 617 Sqn to enable it to commence training for the Dams raid. The following day ED763 was flown to RAF Waddington to become the unit's first Lancaster to be fitted with the special 'Day/Night Flying System' that allowed crews to simulate night flying during the day.

2

Lancaster B III Type 464 Provisioning ED915/AJ-Q, Scampton, April 1943

After arriving at RAF Scampton on 28 April 1943, ED915 was initially allocated to Flt Lt Joe McCarthy RCAF, who christened it QUEENIE CHUCK CHUCK, with an image of a panda carrying a bomb under its arm, licking an ice cream. However, the aircraft was destined not to take part in the Dams raid after an engine failed during start-up. It was not used on any other operations, but was flown on occasional training flights, before being sent to RAF Metheringham in April 1944 and placed in storage. ED915 survived the war, but after the removal of its 'Dambuster' equipment the aircraft was struck off charge on 8 October 1946 and scrapped.

3

Lancaster B III Type 464 Provisioning ED825/AJ-T, Scampton, 16 May 1943

ED825 was the third Lancaster completed to 'Dambuster' specification, and was initially sent to the Aeroplane and Armaments Experimental Establishment (A&AEE) at Boscombe Down. Here, it was used in trials of the underbelly gun position, determining the effects of the modifications on the flying characteristics of the bomber both with and without an Upkeep mine fitted. The aircraft was flown to Scampton on the afternoon of 16 May 1943 to act as a spare, and it was subsequently used on the Dams raid by Flt Lt Joe McCarthy and his crew after their usual mount, ED915/AJ-Q, had suffered an engine failure. By this time the underbelly gun fitted during the trials had been discarded.

4

Lancaster B III Type 464 Provisioning ED825 KC-E, Tempsford, 10 December 1943

After being used on the Dams raid, ED825 was flown by a number of No 617 Sqn crews on training and crew familiarisation sorties. In early November 1943, the aircraft was partially reconverted to near standard configuration, including the installation of a mid-upper turret and bulged bomb-bay doors (allowing it to carry a 12,000-lb HC bomb), and as such was given the new codes KC-E. In this form the Lancaster was flown by Flt Lt Tom O'Shaughnessy's crew on an operation to the Antheor Viaduct on 11 November. Permanently allocated to the crew of Flg Off Gordon Weeden following this mission, ED825 took part in an operation to drop arms and supplies to Resistance forces near Doullons, in France, on 10 December 1943. It was shot down with the loss of all seven on board during the course of this mission. The author was part of a team that excavated the remains of ED825 in November 2007.

5

Lancaster B III Type 464 Provisioning ED912/KC-S, Coningsby, December 1943

Plt Off Les Knight and his crew attacked and breached the Eder Dam in this aircraft on the night of 16-17 May 1943. Over the next few months it was used by a number of crews for both training and further trials, before being one of six 'Dambuster' Lancasters converted to near standard configuration to enable it to carry the 12,000-lb HC bomb, which it took on three further operations in late 1943. ED912's fifth, and final, combat mission was to Belgium on 22 December 1943, when it was armed with 11 1000-lb bombs. The aircraft was prevented from dropping its ordnance by poor weather, which saw the operation abandoned. ED912 remained with No 617 Sqn until the end of the war, when it was flown to a maintenance unit and eventually struck off charge and scrapped in September 1946. The 'Saint' nose art was a regular feature on all the aircraft assigned New Zealand pilot Flt Lt Terry Kearns (who had been allocated the aircraft), this time with the addition of the legend ITMA ('It's That Man Again'), which was the title of a popular radio comedy programme of the day.

6

Lancaster B III Type 464 Provisioning ED909/KC-P, Woodhall Spa, 8 June 1944

ED909 had been flown on the Dams raid by Flt Lt 'Mick' Martin, but despite being reconverted to near standard configuration later that year, it was used operationally only once more during the highly successful attack on the Saumar railway tunnel on 8 June 1944. In addition to bulged bomb-bay doors, the installation of a mid-upper turret and new squadron codes, the aircraft was also fitted with IFF (Identification Friend or Foe) equipment and the H2S radar system, which was housed in a Perspex dome under the fuselage.

7

Lancaster B I DV385/KC-A, Woodhall Spa, mid-1944

DV385 was sent to No 617 Sqn in November 1943, and the aircraft was later fitted with bulged bomb-bay doors to enable it to carry the 12,000-lb HC and Tallboy bombs. DV385 was allocated to Flt Lt Bob Knights upon his posting to the unit, and he added the nose-art THUMPER Mk III (based on the character from the 1942 Disney film Bambi). The mission tally, shown in the form of bombs, included one bearing the letter 'D' for the D-Day spoof raid Operation Taxable, while another featured a swastika to denote the successful shooting down of an enemy fighter by one of the crew's gunners. Having survived the war, DV385 was eventually struck off charge on 11 November 1946 and scrapped.

8

Lancaster B III ED763/KC-Z, Woodhall Spa, November 1944

Having been one of the original ten Lancasters used by No 617 Sqn during its training for the Dams raid, ED763 was later fitted with bulged bomb-bay doors (to enable it to carry the 12,000-lb HC and *Tallboy* bombs) and the SABS (Stabilised Automatic Bomb Sight). Initially recoded KC-D, it became KC-Z in August 1944 and took part in a number of important raids with No 617 Sqn, including all three operations against the *Tirpitz* (for which the mid-upper turret was removed). ED763 was No 617 Sqn's longest-serving aircraft, remaining with the unit until the very end of the war. By then the bomber had flown almost 60 operations. This grand old lady was finally struck off charge in early May 1945 and ignominiously scrapped soon after.

9

Lancaster B III DV393/KC-R, Woodhall Spa, 17 January 1945

DV393 joined No 617 Sqn in early December 1943, flying on its first operation to Flixecourt on the 16th of that month (coded KC-T). Over the next 11 months it completed another 34 raids, including Operation *Taxable* and the first *Tallboy* operation against the Saumar railway tunnel, before being recoded KC-R for its 36th mission – the final decisive raid on the *Tirpitz*. In January 1945, DV393 was one of four aircraft slightly modified to carry a 'Boom Patrol Boat', which it dropped during Operation *Teignmouth II* at Exeter on 17 January 1945 whilst being flown by Flg Off Phil Martin and crew. As well as the boat carriers, additional communication equipment was installed so the crew could remain in contact with the Royal Marine volunteer aboard the boat before the drop. The take-off and flight to the exercise area was made with the bomb-bay doors open due to the size of the boat, which protruded beneath the fuselage – as depicted in this profile. DV393 completed two more operations with No 617 Sqn (on 3 and 6 February) following the boat trials, taking its final mission tally to an impressive 46 in total. The bomber joined No 9 Sqn in March 1945, and having survived the war, it was finally struck off charge on 22 May 1947 and scrapped.

10

Lancaster B I NG228/KC-V, Woodhall Spa, 16 April 1945

NG228 was sent to No 617 Sqn in mid December 1944, and after being allocated the code KC-V, the bomber was flown on its first operation on the 30th of that month (to Ijmuiden). This mission ended up being aborted due to poor weather. Over the next few months the Lancaster embarked on another 14 raids (eight of which were aborted for various reasons), all carrying *Tallboys*, before it was lost during an operation to bomb the German pocket battleship *Lützow* at Swinemünde on 16 April 1945. Carrying 12 1000-lb bombs, NG228 became No 617 Sqn's final combat loss of the war.

11

Lancaster B I (Special) PD112/YZ-S, Woodhall Spa, 14 March 1945

PD112 was one of the first B I (Special) Lancasters to be delivered to No 617 Sqn, this aircraft being part of a batch of just 32 that were constructed to carry the 22,000-lb *Grandslam* bomb. History was made in this machine on 14 March 1945, when it became the first Lancaster to drop a *Grandslam* (then the largest bomb in the world) in action – its target was the Bielefeld Viaduct. Having survived the war, PD112 was struck off charge in March 1948 and scrapped.

12

Lancaster B I (Special) PD113/YZ-T, Woodhall Spa, 19 March 1945

Delivered to No 617 Sqn in early March 1945 with mid-upper and rear turrets, PD113 retained them for its first operation to the Arnsberg Viaduct on 19 March 1945 – this meant it carried a six-man crew, although the mid-upper turret was removed soon after. Built as a B I (Special) to carry a *Grandslam*, PD113 employed the weapon just the once during its eight operations, bombing the U-boat pens at Farge on 27 March 1945. For all of its other missions the aircraft was loaded with a single *Tallboy*. PD113 was finally struck off charge on 6 November 1947 and scrapped soon after.

13

Lancaster B I (Special) PD119/YZ-J, Woodhall Spa, 9 April 1945

After joining No 617 Sqn in March 1945, PD119 immediately became the mount of the unit CO, Grp Capt 'Johnnie' Fauquier. Initially carrying the standard 'night' camouflage scheme, it was soon painted in the 'day' style (the brown and green being slightly lighter than those used in the night scheme), but with a half black/half white outside rudder to indicate that the aircraft was flown by a daylight formation leader. The latter idea proved to be unsuccessful, however, so the unit reverted to an all-black rudder on the outside face instead. After the war PD119 was transferred to No 15 Sqn, where it took part in extensive weapons trials as part of Operation *Front Line*, before it was struck off charge on 20 September 1950 and scrapped.

14

Lancaster B1 (Special) PD121/YZ-Z, Woodhall Spa, 19 April 1945

In a further effort to improve daylight identification between aircraft painted in the day colour scheme, at least one Lancaster (PD121) was repainted with reverse codes of yellow outlined in red – these were also reproduced across the bomber's tail surfaces. PD121 joined No 617 Sqn in mid-March 1945, and flew on six operations (four carrying a *Tallboy*) before VE Day. Later passed on to No 15 Sqn, where it too participated in Operation *Front Line*, the bomber was reduced to scrap after being struck off charge on 19 May 1947.

15

Lancaster B III Type 464 Provisioning ED909 of the Station Flight, Scampton, October 1946

Having been converted to near standard configuration after the Dams raid (in which guise it was used operationally on 8 June 1944), ED909 was restored to its modified 'Dambuster' state in August 1944 and flown to RAF Metheringham for storage. In January 1945, along with the rest of the surviving 'Dambuster' aircraft, it was transferred to No 46 MU, were it remained for almost 18 months. When three Lancasters were required to participate in Operation *Guzzle*, ED909 was one of those hastily refurbished and flown to RAF Scampton, seemingly with its former codes painted over. With *Guzzle* having been completed by the end of December 1946, the bomber remained at RAF Scampton and was duly allocated to the Station Flight with the new codes YF-B. Initially earmarked as a ground instructional airframe in mid-January 1947, the veteran bomber's status was later cancelled and ED909 was instead struck off charge and scrapped at Scampton in July of that year.

16

Lancaster Type 464 Provisioning ED906/YF-A of the Station Flight, Scampton, October 1946

ED906 was yet another *Guzzle* aircraft, having originally been flown on the Dams raid by Flt Lt David Maltby as AJ-J. Between November 1943 and the start of January 1944, it was used on a further five operations, having been partially reconverted to a near standard configuration and coded KC-J. Later sent to RAF Metheringham for storage (having had its 'Dambuster' components restored and codes changed to AJ-G), ED906 was used for various duties by No 106 Sqn personnel and No 54 Base test crews from RAF Coningsby, before being sent to No 46 MU in June 1945. Selected as one of three aircraft to be refurbished for Operation *Guzzle*, the bomber was then flown to Scampton in mid-August 1946 whilst still marked up with its AJ-G codes from its time with No 617 Sqn. After the operation was completed, ED906 was allocated to the RAF Scampton Station Flight with the codes YF–A, before finally being struck off charge in July 1947 and broken up on site soon afterwards.

17

Lancaster B VII (FE) NX782/KC-T, Digri, India, January-April 1946

NX782 was one of the Lancasters intended for use by No 617 Sqn in the Far East as part of the stillborn Tiger Force. Carrying this colour scheme, it was instead flown during the deployment to India in early 1946. The Mk VII (FE) Lancaster was instantly recognisable thanks to its electrically-powered Martin mid-upper turret (situated further forward than usual), which replaced the standard hydraulic Frazer-Nash turret, and a Frazer-Nash 82 rear turret. Both were fitted with 0.5-in machine guns instead of the earlier 0.303-in weapons. This aircraft was also featured in the 1955 feature film *The Dam Busters*, albeit in standard configuration, as Guy Gibson's No 106 Sqn aircraft.

18

Mosquito FB IV DZ525/AZ-S of No 627 Sqn, Woodhall Spa, June 1944

Mosquito DZ525 was one of a number borrowed by No 617 Sqn from neighbouring No 627 Sqn for marking duties prior to the unit receiving its own aircraft. A fighter-bomber version, it was used just once operationally by No 617 Sqn for the operation to Wizernes on 22 June 1944 – it was flown by Flt Lt Gerry Fawke and his navigator Flg Off Tom Bennett on this mission. DZ525 survived the war and was struck off charge in September 1945.

19

Mosquito B IV DZ641/AZ-C of No 627 Sqn, Woodhall Spa, June 1944

No 627 Sqn was using a variety of colour schemes in mid-1944, with aircraft flying on operations both by day and by night. DZ641, a bomber version with bulged bomb-bay doors, is seen here in a standard night camouflage scheme, but with the addition of full 'invasion stripes' around the fuselage and under the wings. These were intended to help Allied forces on the ground quickly identify friendly aircraft overhead, and they were ordered to be applied to all aircraft from 4 June 1944 – just in time for D-Day. Sqn Ldr David Shannon and his navigator, Flg Off Len Sumpter, flew DZ641 to Wizernes on 22 June 1944. It survived the war and was struck off charge in January 1946.

20

Mosquito FB VI NS993/N, Woodhall Spa, April 1944

NS993 was one of only four Mosquitos actually assigned to No 617 Sqn. None of them carried the unit's code letters, however, relying on a single individual identifying letter instead. After his initial Mosquito operation in ML976/HS–N, borrowed from No 109 Sqn, Leonard Cheshire settled on NS993 as his regular mount. Indeed, he flew it on 11 occasions between mid-April and late June 1944, before handing it over to new squadron commander 'Willie' Tait, who flew it a further five times. It would seem that although the squadron Mosquitos were allocated AJ codes on paper, in reality they only carried a single identification letter (as both the AJ and KC codes were in use on No 617 Sqn Lancasters at the same time). NS993 was later handed over to No 515 Sqn, and it was flying with this unit when it force-landed in Switzerland on 30 September 1944. The Swiss impounded the aircraft and later used it themselves, before it was finally destroyed in a crash in early 1950.

21

Mustang III HB839, Woodhall Spa, 6 July 1944

HB839 was one of two brand new Mustang IIIs sent to No 617 Sqn for marking purposes on 22 June 1944. Fitted with the Spitfire-style 'Malcolm' hood (an RAF modification), this aircraft was officially assigned the code letter N, although in reality this does not seem to have been applied. Fully armed, the fighter was last used operationally on the 4 August 1944 mission to Etaples (when flown by Wg Cdr 'Willie' Tait). It remained with No 617 Sqn until 2 October, when it was sent to No 30 MU, along with its sister HB825. HB839 later saw service with both Nos 541 and 309 Sqns, before being struck off charge in March 1947 and scrapped.

BIBLIOGRAPHY

ARTHUR, MAX, *Dambusters – A Landmark Oral History,* Virgin, 2008

BENNETT, TOM, *617 Squadron – Dambusters at War,* Patrick Stephens Limited, 1986

BOYLE, ANDREW, *No Passing Glory – The Full and Authentic Biography of Group Captain Cheshire VC, DSO, DFC,* Collins, 1955

BRICKHILL, PAUL, *The Dam Busters,* Evans Brothers, 1951

BURGESS, COLIN, *Australia's Dambusters,* Australian Military History Publications (AMHP), 2003

BURKE, EDMUND, *Guy Gibson VC,* Arco, 1961

COOPER, ALAN, *The Men Who Breached The Dams,* William Kimber, 1982

COOPER, ALAN, *Beyond The Dams To The Tirpitz,* William Kimber, 1983

COOPER, ALAN, *Born Leader – The Story of Guy Gibson VC,* Independent Books, 1993

COOPER, ALAN, *The Dambusters Squadron – Fifty Years of 617 Squadron RAF,* Arms & Armour Press, 1993

DRIESSCHEN, JAN VAN DEN, *We Will Remember Them,* The Erskine Press, 2004

EULER, HELMUTH, *Als Deutschlands Damme Brachen,* Motor Buch Verlag, 1987

EULER, HELMUTH, *The Dams Raid Through The Lens,* After the Battle, 2001

FALCONER, JONATHAN, *The Dam Busters – Breaking The Dams of Western Germany 16–17 May 1943,* Sutton, 2003

FALCONER, JONATHAN, *Filming The Dambusters,* Sutton, 2005

FOSTER, CHARLES, *Breaking The Dams,* Pen & Sword, 2008

FRY, ERIC, *An Airman Far Away,* Kangaroo Press, 1993

GIBSON, GUY, *Enemy Coast Ahead,* Michael Joseph Ltd, 1946

HARRISON, SIMON, *Dambusters – The 60th Anniversary,* Royal Air Force Museum, 2003

HILLIER, SQN LDR S J, *The History of 617 Squadron 'The Dambusters' 1943–1993,* Forces and Corporate Publishing, 1993

HUMPHRIES, HARRY, *Living With Heroes – The Dam Busters,* The Erskine Press, 2003

KELLOW, BOB, *Paths to Freedom,* Kellow Corporation, 1992

LAWRENCE, W J, *No 5 Bomber Group RAF,* Faber, 1951

MASON, FRANCIS K, *The Avro Lancaster,* Aston, 1989

MORRIS, RICHARD, *Guy Gibson,* Viking, 1994

MORRIS, RICHARD, *Cheshire – The Biography of Leonard Cheshire,* Viking, 2000

OTTAWAY, SUSAN, *Dambuster – A Life of Guy Gibson VC,* Leo Cooper, 1994

POSTLETHWAITE, MARK, *Dambusters in Focus,* Red Kite, 2007

SIMPSON, TOM, *Lower Than Low,* Libra, 1995

SWEETMAN, JOHN, *The Dambusters Raid,* Cassell, 1999

SWEETMAN, JOHN, *The Dambusters,* Time Warner, 2003

SWEETMAN, JOHN, *Tirpitz – Hunting The Beast,* The History Press Ltd, 2004

THORNING, ARTHUR, *The Dambuster Who Cracked The Dam,* Pen & Sword, 2008

WARD, CHRIS, *Dambusters – The Definitive History of 617 Squadron at War 1943–1945,* Red Kite, 2003 & 2008

WARD, CHRIS, *Dambuster Raid Crash Sites,* Pen & Sword, 2007

WOODWARD, DAVID, *The Tirpitz and the Battle for the North Atlantic,* Berkley Books, 1953